W9-BYF-690

Thank you for returning
your books on time.

INTRODUCING
ISSUES WITH
OPPOSING
VIEWPOINTS®

Standardized Testing

Cynthia A. Bily, *Book Editor*

GREENHAVEN PRESS
A part of Gale, Cengage Learning

GALE
CENGAGE Learning

Detroit • New York • San Francisco • New Haven, Conn • Waterville, Maine • London

GALE
CENGAGE Learning™

Christine Nasso, *Publisher*
Elizabeth Des Chenes, *Managing Editor*

© 2011 Greenhaven Press, a part of Gale, Cengage Learning

Gale and Greenhaven Press are registered trademarks used herein under license.

For more information, contact:
Greenhaven Press
27500 Drake Rd.
Farmington Hills, MI 48331-3535
Or you can visit our Internet site at gale.cengage.com

For product information and technology assistance, contact us at

Gale Customer Support, 1-800-877-4253
For permission to use material from this text or product, submit all requests online at www.cengage.com/permissions

Further permissions questions can be e-mailed to permissionrequest@cengage.com

Articles in Greenhaven Press anthologies are often edited for length to meet page requirements. In addition, original titles of these works are changed to clearly present the main thesis and to explicitly indicate the author's opinion. Every effort is made to ensure that Greenhaven Press accurately reflects the original intent of the authors. Every effort has been made to trace the owners of copyrighted material.

Cover: © Spencer Grant/Alamy.

LIBRARY OF CONGRESS CATALOGING-IN-PUBLICATION DATA
Standardized testing / Cynthia A. Bily, book editor.   p. cm. -- (Introducing issues with opposing viewpoints) Includes bibliographical references and index. ISBN 978-0-7377-5202-1 (hardcover) 1. Educational tests and measurements--United States. I. Bily, Cynthia A. LB3051.S787 2011 371.26'2--dc22 <div align="right">2010037588</div>

Printed in the United States of America
1 2 3 4 5 6 7 15 14 13 12 11

Contents

Chapter 3: Are Standardized Tests Valuable for College Admissions?

Foreword

I ndulging in a wide spectrum of ideas, beliefs, and perspectives is a critical cornerstone of democracy. After all, it is often debates over differences of opinion, such as whether to legalize abortion, how to treat prisoners, or when to enact the death penalty, that shape our society and drive it forward. Such diversity of thought is frequently regarded as the hallmark of a healthy and civilized culture. As the Reverend Clifford Schutjer of the First Congregational Church in Mansfield, Ohio, declared in a 2001 sermon, "Surrounding oneself with only like-minded people, restricting what we listen to or read only to what we find agreeable is irresponsible. Refusing to entertain doubts once we make up our minds is a subtle but deadly form of arrogance." With this advice in mind, Introducing Issues with Opposing Viewpoints books aim to open readers' minds to the critically divergent views that compose our world's most important debates.

Introducing Issues with Opposing Viewpoints simplifies for students the enormous and often overwhelming mass of material now available via print and electronic media. Collected in every volume is an array of opinions that captures the essence of a particular controversy or topic. Introducing Issues with Opposing Viewpoints books embody the spirit of nineteenth-century journalist Charles A. Dana's axiom: "Fight for your opinions, but do not believe that they contain the whole truth, or the only truth." Absorbing such contrasting opinions teaches students to analyze the strength of an argument and compare it to its opposition. From this process readers can inform and strengthen their own opinions or be exposed to new information that will change their minds. Introducing Issues with Opposing Viewpoints is a mosaic of different voices. The authors are statesmen, pundits, academics, journalists, corporations, and ordinary people who have felt compelled to share their experiences and ideas in a public forum. Their words have been collected from newspapers, journals, books, speeches, interviews, and the Internet, the fastest growing body of opinionated material in the world.

Introducing Issues with Opposing Viewpoints shares many of the well-known features of its critically acclaimed parent series, Opposing Viewpoints. The articles are presented in a pro/con format, allowing readers to absorb divergent perspectives side by side. Active reading questions preface each viewpoint, requiring the student to approach the material thoughtfully and carefully. Useful charts, graphs, and cartoons supplement each article. A thorough introduction provides readers with crucial background on an issue. An annotated bibliography points the reader toward articles, books, and websites that contain additional information on the topic. An appendix of organizations to contact contains a wide variety of charities, nonprofit organizations, political groups, and private enterprises that each hold a position on the issue at hand. Finally, a comprehensive index allows readers to locate content quickly and efficiently.

Introducing Issues with Opposing Viewpoints is also significantly different from Opposing Viewpoints. As the series title implies, its presentation will help introduce students to the concept of opposing viewpoints, and teach them to use this material to aid in critical writing and debate. The series' four-color, accessible format makes the books attractive and inviting to readers of all levels. In addition, each viewpoint has been carefully edited to maximize readers understanding of the content. Short but thorough viewpoints capture the essence of an argument. A substantial, thought-provoking essay question placed at the end of each viewpoint asks students to further investigate the issues raised in the viewpoint, compare and contrast two authors' arguments, or consider how one might go about forming an opinion on the topic at hand. Each viewpoint contains sidebars that include at-a-glance information and handy statistics. A Facts About section located in the back of the book further supplies students with relevant facts and figures.

Following in the tradition of the Opposing Viewpoints series, Greenhaven Press continues to provide readers with invaluable exposure to the controversial issues that shape our world. As John Stuart Mill once wrote: "The only way in which a human being can make some approach to knowing the whole of a subject is by hearing what can be said about it by persons of every variety of opinion and studying all modes in which it can be looked at by every character of mind. No wise man ever acquired his wisdom in any mode but this." It is to this principle that Introducing Issues with Opposing Viewpoints books are dedicated.

Introduction

At this defining moment in our history, preparing our children to compete in the global economy is one of the most urgent challenges we face. We need to stop paying lip service to public education, and start holding communities, administrators, teachers, parents and students accountable.
—Barack Obama, Organizing for America, BarackObama.com

In the current debate over how to improve education in the United States, one of the guiding words is *accountability*. For too long, many people believe, American schoolchildren—especially poor children, children of color, children with disabilities, children from unstable homes, and children who are learning to speak English—have been subject to an educational system that has not met their needs, and many children have been moved along from grade to grade without learning essential skills. This has happened, the thinking goes, because no one had been held accountable for the children—that is, no one had been made to report on the progress each child makes, and no one had faced consequences when children did not learn. But in his 2007 State of the Union address, President George W. Bush celebrated the improvements made under the No Child Left Behind Act (NCLB), which was passed by Congress in the year 2000 with the goals of "preserving local control, raising standards in public schools, and holding those schools accountable for results."

Accountability has shaped education reform since the end of the twentieth century, as policy makers, educators, and parents have worked to measure learning. In 1999, Harvard professor of education Richard F. Elmore wrote that "accountability for student performance is one of the two or three—if not the most—prominent issues in policy at the state and local levels right now." Education World, a website that provides information for teachers, carries articles with titles including "Adjusting to Accountability in the Days of NCLB," "From the Principal Files: Has Accountability Taken All the Fun Out of Teaching and Learning?" and "Driven by Data—What It's Like to

Teach in the Age of Accountability." Research and advocacy organizations, including the National Center for Educational Accountability, the National Center for Special Education Accountability, and New York's Foundation for Education Reform and Accountability, have led the discussion.

A Google search for "accountability education" yields more than 37 million hits, demonstrating a wide range of interested people. Parents want to know whether their children are learning what they should be learning. Taxpayers want to know whether their tax dollars, which fund public schools, are being used wisely. Lawmakers want to know whether the schools in their districts are doing everything they should be doing to help children face the future. And everyone wants to know whom to blame—whom to hold accountable—for the students who are falling behind.

The word *accountable* has the word *count* within it, and people looking for accountability generally look for something to count—numbers, data—as they determine which states, which school districts, which schools, or which teachers are teaching children well. In most cases, this data is gathered by having students take standardized tests, or tests given to large numbers of students under consistent or "standard" conditions. Advocates argue that they are the best way to compare students from different schools and different times—to learn whether a third grader in Minnesota in 2010 has learned as much about math as a third grader in Florida in 2007. "By testing every child," Bush said in his 2004 Republican nomination speech, "we are identifying those who need help and providing a record level of funding. Challenging the soft bigotry of low expectations is the spirit of our education reform, and the commitment of our country: . . .We will leave no child behind."

Opponents of these tests argue that they rely too much on multiple-choice questions that do not demand real thinking and that too much pressure is put on teachers to "teach to the test." Many educators, while acknowledging the moral obligation to find out which students need more help, have questioned whether standardized tests provide that information, and they have called for new ways to find out what students can do. Barack Obama, in a 2008 article on Education.com written while he was still a candidate for the presidency, promised to "provide funds for states to implement a broader range of assessments that can evaluate higher-order skills, including students' abilities to use technology, conduct research, engage in scientific investigation, solve problems, [and] present and defend their ideas."

Although the roles of standardized tests have changed over time, what has not changed is the controversy over how best to help students learn and how to measure that learning. Teachers disagree about whether the tests fairly show whether they are doing their jobs well, policy makers disagree about whether the tests can help them know when to become involved in shaping education, researchers disagree about whether the tests help or hurt what goes on in the classroom, and college admissions officers and employers disagree about whether standardized test results really tell them what they need to know about applicants. As people of good will work to determine the best ways to determine whether students' needs are being met, they must struggle with three important questions: Does standardized testing increase learning? Does standardized testing benefit teachers? Is standardized testing valuable for college admission? The authors of the following viewpoints debate both sides of these questions.

Chapter 1

Does Standardized Testing Increase Learning?

All students must take standardized tests throughout their school years.

Standardized Testing Helps Identify Student Needs

Karen Tankersley

"Although the tests may seem isolated and un-related to the overarching goals of instruction in the class-room, nothing could be further from the truth."

In the following viewpoint, reading education expert Karen Tankersley explains how teachers can use the standardized tests that their students must take to shape their teaching. Contrary to what many people think, the tests demand complex thinking from students, she contends, and a good teacher will teach complex thinking skills, not merely the memorization of facts. Students who have been taught well will do well on the tests, she argues, and weaknesses in students' performances show teachers exactly which skills students still need to work on. A former classroom teacher and principal, Tankersley is a professor of educational leadership at Arizona State University.

AS YOU READ, CONSIDER THE FOLLOWING QUESTIONS:
1. How many of the multiple-choice questions described by the author in her example ask students literally to recall information stated directly in the test passage?
2. What should teachers do after they have designed a student activity, according to Tankersley?
3. What does the author mean by the term "circular link" as applied to assessments in U.S. education?

If we are to help our students become independent and deep thinkers, we must change our view of our role in the process. We must abandon the view of a teacher as the keeper and dispenser of knowledge and move to a model where teaching means observing and diagnosing students' current level of performance and then providing guidance that can help them advance their skills and understandings to the next level. While there is no question that knowledge is important, what makes the difference is the ability to locate the appropriate information and then process and apply that information at the right time and in the right way. Many state standards require higher-level thinking and reasoning skills. If we are to help students acquire learning for life, rather than just pass a test, we must raise the performance bar beyond mere memorization.

One of the reasons that many teachers balk at what they term "teaching to the test" is because they cannot see past the "individual" or minute skills that they believe state assessments require of students. They have difficulty connecting the seemingly disjointed questions to the broader curriculum and the standards they have been asked to teach. Although the tests may seem isolated and unrelated to the overarching goals of instruction in the classroom, nothing could be further from the truth. The skills that students need to perform well on constructed-response or problem-based assessments are actually much more complex than what might be first perceived. Because state-released items are meant to provide teachers with a guide of what the actual state test will be like, we can examine a sample question to test this idea.

Let's consider the issue of complexity by looking at a sample assessment question from the released items on the Department of Education Web site for the 8th grade language arts test from Massachusetts. On the selected sample item, students are asked to read a three-paragraph excerpt from "A Walk to the Jetty" from *Annie John* by Jamaica Kincaid. Students then have seven multiple-choice questions and one constructed-response item based on this short passage. Using this one text passage, let's see what understandings and skills students need to respond to this question.

Higher-Order Thinking Is Required
When we categorize the seven multiple-choice questions, we see that one question directly asks for an interpretation of how a word is used in the passage, one asks students to identify the part of speech of a word in a sentence, one asks students to determine the author's word choice in a specific sentence, one requires literal recall of information directly stated in the passage, and the remaining three questions ask students to choose a response by making an inference. Clearly, the expectation is that students will demonstrate higher-order thinking,

Standardized testing can reveal a student's weaknesses, allowing a teacher to help the student work on specfic areas.

because six of the seven questions require higher-order processing skills to some degree.

If I am an 8th grade language arts teacher hoping to prepare my students for success on this assessment, it is clear that my students must be well prepared to draw inferences from text, analyze and discuss the author's word choice, and demonstrate the ability to interpret vocabulary meaning from context. We can learn all this from analyzing just one sample question.

Continuing our analysis of this sample item, we then find a constructed-response question addressing this same text passage: "Identify and explain the mixed feelings the speaker has about leaving her home. Use relevant and specific information from the excerpt to support your answer." Again, not only must students be able to identify passage tone, but they must also be able to "interpret" and draw conclusions about the writer's attitudes and emotions from the text. Once students have identified these important concepts, they must then "cite evidence" to support their conclusions as well as construct a meaningful, well-organized essay to convey their ideas. Classroom instruction must help students learn to interpret a writer's viewpoint and draw a conclusion, compose a quality essay, and link meaningful passages to provide support for ideas and conclusions. Again, these are complex concepts for most 8th grade students. . . .

Linking Instruction with Assessment

Taking language arts as an example, let's think about the ways students are assessed. Since we know that state tests will require students to analyze aspects of text, we might ask them to read a poem and write a couple of paragraphs describing how the author used imagery in the poem. If we know that students are often asked to read a short text excerpt and compare and contrast two characters, we could design activities that ask our students to do exactly that. If we want to extend

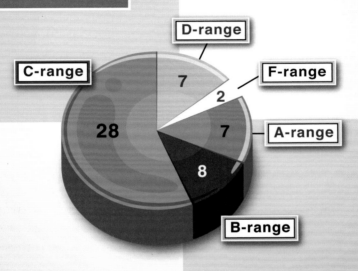

The Rigor of State Standards

Paul E. Peterson and Carlos Xabel Lastra-Anadón of Harvard University evaluated the rigor of states' eighth-grade reading proficiency standards in 2009, giving each state a letter grade. Massachusetts, the state mentioned in the viewpoint, earned an "A." Numbers indicate the number of states receiving the grade indicated by the color.

D-range — 7

C-range — 28

F-range — 2

A-range — 7

B-range — 8

Taken from: Paul E. Peterson and Carlos Xabel Lastra-Anádon, "State Standards Rising in Reading, but Not in Math," *Education Next*, Fall 2010. http://educationnext.org/state-standards-rising-in-reading-but-not-in-math.

that process into a longer instructional time frame, we might ask students to read two stories or two novels and then compare and contrast them. The format of the task should mirror the segment that students will be expected to do on the state assessment but in a more complex form. We will use this opportunity to guide and shape instruction as well as to provide feedback on student performance.

Once you have designed a student activity, the next step is to take the assessment yourself or ask a colleague in your area to take the assessment for you and give you feedback. As you respond, try to view the task from your students' perspective. Although responses will vary, try to identify as many possible answers or ways of solving the problem as might be acceptable. What are some of the difficulties your students might have? Can you eliminate these problems by reworking your prompt or task? Taking the test yourself will help you spot potential trouble spots so that you can rework the item to improve it. When we know our students can perform a comparison on a longer, more complex work—as in this example—we also know that they can do the same task on a brief text passage that may appear on the state exam. When our instruction is at the more complex level, state assessments become easy tasks for our students, and they perform well. . . .

Assessments are truly the circular link that tells us where to start our instruction, how much students have learned, and how much they still need to learn to demonstrate mastery. Since state tests and high-accountability measures are a reality in U.S. education, we must actively find ways to work more efficiently. We do that by clearly understanding what students are expected to do, sharing and collaborating with our peers, and helping students take responsibility for their own performance and improvement. With this change, we can truly deepen student thinking and become the wizard behind the curtain directing learning from behind the scenes.

EVALUATING THE AUTHOR'S ARGUMENTS:

The viewpoint you have just read is one of several in this book written by someone who has been a teacher; others were written by reporters, researchers, advocates, and administrators—people who may or may not work with children every day. Who is best qualified to determine what students need and how best to provide for their needs? Why? Using what you have read, how should a district, state, or nation balance the opinions of educators, businesspeople, researchers, advocates, politicians, and students to establish its educational policies?

Standardized Testing Restricts Student Learning

Helen Cole, Kathy Hulley, and Peggy Quarles

"Standardized testing results often create a narrowly taught curriculum because these test results are considered "high stakes" measurements."

In the following viewpoint, Helen Cole, Kathy Hulley, and Peggy Quarles examine how teachers' needs to produce good scores on standardized tests affect what they teach their students. Because the tests generally ask questions that have one correct answer, the authors contend they force teachers to emphasize memorization rather than more complex thinking skills. Schools must develop and use strategies to assess students' performance in more sophisticated activities, they conclude. The authors are members of the graduate faculty in teacher education at Lincoln Memorial University in Tennessee.

Helen Cole, Kathy Hulley, and Peggy Quarles, "Does Assessment Have to Drive Curriculum?" *Forum on Public Policy*, Spring 2009. Reproduced by permission.

AS YOU READ, CONSIDER THE FOLLOWING QUESTIONS:
1. According to Swope and Miner, as cited by the authors, what should be the goal of assessment?
2. As described by Cole, Hulley, and Quarles, what has happened to the curriculum in Great Britain's schools?
3. Instead of standardized tests, what kinds of activities, as suggested by the authors, would give students and teachers a better sense of what students have learned?

In the real estate market the key word is location, location, location. In education the key word is assessment, assessment, assessment. Do we need all the assessment? What is the purpose behind all the assessment in our schools? Assessment is a concern not only in our schools in the United States, but in British schools as well. Are teachers to teach to the test? Are the tests an accurate reflection of a level of intelligence or merely a reflection of what a student can recall or know? What about authentic assessment, does it have a place in our schools? Are we testing what our students will be able to do in the world as citizens or are we testing them to see what they can merely recall?

According to Bloom's Taxonomy [of learning objectives], recalling facts is at the lower end of the spectrum of critical thinking skills. Application and synthesis of knowledge reside at the top of Bloom's Taxonomy. Are we doing our students a disservice in our assessment of their knowledge? Are we restricting classroom activities, projects, and other hands-on activities for the sake of the test? How do we answer these questions as teachers? As administrators? As school districts? As nations? Are we truly assessing our students' abilities in the real world in which they live?

There is a heavy emphasis on testing to measure what students are/are not mastering in the content areas. Testing, according to Paul Ramsey, a representative of Educational Testing Service, "must provide accurate, valid, and reliable measurement of student knowledge. These tests must be aligned with the curriculum. If tests are not aligned with the curriculum, the test cannot be a valid measure for standards-based accountability." . . .

Striking a Balance

Ramsey advocates "adequate opportunities for students to learn the material that will be tested and . . . the format of the test that will be used." We need a balance between classroom and large scale assessment. According to [Louis] Volante, the most timely and relevant type of assessment data is "integrating a range of curriculum-embedded assessment measures for accountability purposes, focusing attention when it is needed most—improving reliability and validity of classroom assessment data." [Kathy] Swope [and Barbara] Miner agree that the goal of assessment should be "to help students learn and to provide them a quality education—not to constantly compare schools and children."

So, does teaching to the test drive the curriculum? Volante answers with an emphatic "yes." Research has documented that teaching to

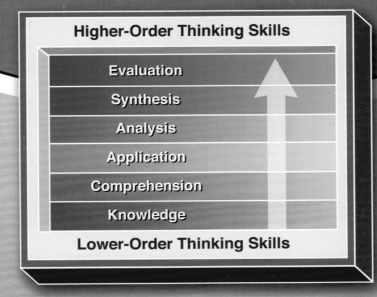

Bloom's Taxonomy

In 1956 Benjamin Bloom and his colleagues created what is known as "Bloom's Taxonomy," a visual representation of the complexity of the skills needed for learning and critical thinking.

Higher-Order Thinking Skills

Evaluation
Synthesis
Analysis
Application
Comprehension
Knowledge

Lower-Order Thinking Skills

Taken from: Benjamin Bloom, ed., *The Taxonomy of Educational Objectives: The Classification of Educational Goals, Handbook I; Cognitive Domain.* Susan Fauer Company, 1956.

the test does raise test scores, but what is the overall effect on the student population? He also asks the question, "Is there application from these tests to the real world?" However, Swope and Miner believe that "standardized tests will never answer the questions of what our children need to learn to be leaders and informed citizens in a multicultural, ever-changing world." Standardized testing results often create a narrowly taught curriculum because these test results are considered "high stakes" measurements.

Just what is the history of standardized testing? In the past standardized testing or IQ tests were used to sort children mostly along racial and class lines. The latest form of standardized testing is getting similar results. Standardized tests can actually determine teaching and learning in ways that can harm children. Standardized tests only test factual knowledge (recall) and not aspects of thinking and learning. The more schools use standardized tests, the more the curriculum becomes standardized. According to Harold Berlak as quoted [by] Swope and Miner, state-mandated standards and tests "are an effort to put an end to the most valuable asset of views about what constitutes truth, knowledge, and learning. . . . Standardized curriculum and tests insist upon one set of answers and only one."

Narrowing the Curriculum

According to Melissa Schieble, the National Curriculum in Britain has significantly narrowed what can be taught and has reinforced . . . a skill-and-drill approach to schooling. It is virtually impossible to avoid when there's such an emphasis on examination results and classroom teachers are held accountable for students' test scores. Prince Charles made headlines regarding the National Curriculum and examinations: "I want to encourage teachers to enrich their teaching despite the straitjacket of assessment." And he continued, "More frequent exams mean that the time for learning has shrunk and that leads to defensive teaching." Yet, Ramsey, the Educational Testing Services representative states, "The NCLB [No Child Left Behind Act] in the U.S. and the ECM (Every Child Matters in England) learning standards are mandated, measured, and tracked and by law require annual assessment." He even goes on to say that "Tests are a necessary component of standards-based education reform but they are not sufficient within themselves." He believes that teachers must have training in "appropriate methods for standards-based teaching." There must be clear articulation between standards and standards-based testing. All stakeholders must be informed and educated about the assessment procedure. . . .

What can be done to rectify this assessment problem? The U.S. and England are both multicultural countries. Therefore, how do we envision a marriage between standardized assessment and multicultural education? After all, testing is only one part of the educational pie. . . .

Authentic Assessments

What is best for students is performance-based assessments—essays, research projects, science experiments, or work that shows student progress over time, such as portfolios. Many educators are confused about just how to go about all this assessment. In Georgia, teachers are required to use GPS (Georgia Performance Standards) yet in the actual testing process, standardized tests are used, which only ask for knowledge or facts that students can merely recall, not apply. Another caveat—standardized tests are given on school days, usually taking two to three hours for each testing session. Do we really have time that we can take away from the curriculum? Another point to consider with the standardized-tests driven curriculum is that it often sets the bar low for achievement. Often the curriculum gets "dumbed down" to teach to the test. . . .

The ultimate objective for assessment should be to put authentic teaching and learning at the forefront of efforts to reform assessment policies and practice. Authentic assessment/performance assessments simulate real-life tasks. Authentic assessment tests for application and synthesis, which require a higher level of thinking skills. Volante states that "Effectiveness [of assessment] should be understood as a product of authentic teaching and learning that focus on the demonstration of higher-order thinking skills and knowledge transfer." Volante states, and we agree, that "Failure to balance our assessment methods leads to predictable negative consequences for students, teachers, and the school system in general."

EVALUATING THE AUTHORS' ARGUMENTS:

The viewpoint you have just read makes a distinction between "intelligence" and "what a student can recall or know." Based on your experience as a student, do you think these qualities are separate? Do they have different uses in the world outside school? How can a school measure how intelligent students are, as opposed to how much they have learned? *Should* the education system make this distinction? Why or why not?

Standardized Testing Has Improved Education for Poor and Minority Students

Education Equality Project

"Strength-ened account-ability over the last decade is associated with improved student achievement, especially for low-income and minority students."

In the following viewpoint, the Education Equality Project argues that standardized testing is bringing a new level of fairness and equality to public education in the United States. Before the law known as No Child Left Behind (NCLB), the author claims, it was easy for schools to deliver poor education to students—particularly to poor and minority students—without being noticed. The standardized testing required by NCLB, the author concludes, forces teachers, schools, districts, and states to deliver an equal education to all students.

The Education Equality Project is a group of elected officials, civil rights leaders, and

"ESEA Backgrounder 1: Accountability Systems," Education Equality Project, March 3, 2010. Reproduced by permission.

education reformers who work to eliminate the racial and ethnic achievement gap in public education.

AS YOU READ, CONSIDER THE FOLLOWING QUESTIONS:

1. Under the terms of No Child Left Behind, for which groups of students do states have to gather achievement data, according to the author?
2. According to the Education Equality Project, how have good grades harmed many poor and minority students?
3. What evidence does the author present to support the claim that standardized testing has helped nine-year-olds learn to read?

Testing and accountability provisions have existed in ESEA [the Elementary and Secondary Education Act] since 1965. Prior to 1994, however, these guidelines were vague and unenforced. This changed with the passage of President [Bill] Clinton's Goals 2000 Act and 1994 ESEA reauthorization, which required each state to: (1) develop academic standards, (2) create and administer annual assessments aligned to those standards (once each in grades 3–5, 6–8, and 10–11), and (3) develop a system of adequate yearly progress (AYP) by which to judge student attainment of state academic standards. Few states, however, set clear goals or reported separately on the progress of at-risk groups.

The 2002 reauthorization of ESEA—NCLB [No Child Left Behind]—made three key changes to ESEA accountability requirements:

1. States would have to disaggregate student achievement data within each state, local education agency, and school by gender, racial and ethnic group, and English proficiency status, and for immigrants, students with disabilities, and economically disadvantaged students.
2. States would have to set AYP goals for closing achievement gaps between students in the above at-risk subgroups and their peers by 2014. Local education agencies and schools would be held accountable for meeting their annual objectives (e.g., increasing the percentage of students proficient in reading from 50 percent to 55 percent).

3. Testing would be required annually in reading and math in grades 3–8.

NCLB also required all states to participate in the National Assessment of Educational Progress (NAEP), the nation's report card, as a check on state test results. (Several states had previously not participated in NAEP.)

Rationale for Standardized Testing

History shows that poor and minority students are generally held to lower standards than their peers. They are often told they are doing "fine," and they receive good grades and ultimately high school diplomas —only to graduate from high school and discover that they don't have the knowledge and skills needed to succeed in college and/or the workplace. Intentional or not, biases in the system frequently mask failure until it is too late to remediate.

To understand whether or not students—regardless of race, income, national origin, disability, or ZIP code—have access to a high-quality education, states realized they need a fair way of assessing school performance. Policymakers need a valid way to determine whether

Kindergartners take a computer test at school. The No Child Left Behind Act requires standardized testing.

all students are being held to the same high standards and to compare students' achievement of those standards across schools, districts, and states. Standardized tests are the only truly objective and scientifically valid way to make these critical comparisons. In recognition of this, in 1989, the National Governors Association (NGA), led by then-Governor Clinton and supported by President George H.W. Bush, launched an initiative for new state standards and assessments, which was then codified into federal law in 1994 and accompanied by $2 billion in start-up and implementation funding over the next six years. It is critical to note that states use this information to guide their decision-making and policy-setting on all fronts—funding; curricula; supports and interventions for students, teachers, and schools; etc. States are not collecting data to collect data; they are using this information to improve their education systems.

Whether or not we continue to obtain information from standardized tests and use it to inform policy decisions from the White House to the classroom will have serious, long-term implications for students. If we revert to a patchwork of standards and assessments that vary according to political pressure or societal and community biases, historically disadvantaged students, whether intentionally or unintentionally, will be mislabeled as achieving high standards when in fact they are not. In turn, the schools in which poor and minority students are enrolled are likely to be overlooked when it comes to badly needed investments in teaching and learning and in formulating and implementing fundamental reforms in chronically failing schools. . . .

Data Crucial to Finding Achievement Gaps

Before the passage of NCLB, state and local accountability systems typically analyzed and published student achievement data based only on average student achievement. This type of reporting hid critical information about subgroups of students—particularly gaps between their achievement and that of their more advantaged peers. Federal law requires that student achievement data be disaggregated by race, ethnicity, gender, disability status, migrant status, English proficiency, and status as economically disadvantaged.

(Note: School lunch is used most often, but not always, to measure economic disadvantage.)

Prior to 2002:
- Only 11 states disaggregated (i.e., analyzed, compared, and reported) achievement data by gender or ethnicity;
- Only six states disaggregated for economically disadvantaged students;
- Only seven states disaggregated for English proficiency status;
- Only one state disaggregated for migrant students; and
- Only one state (Texas) had a state goal of narrowing or closing achievement gaps between any of these groups. . . .

Ambitious Goals and Timelines

A number of rigorous research studies have demonstrated that strengthened accountability over the last decade is associated with improved student achievement, especially for low-income and minority students.

A majority of states have seen improvements in overall student achievement and a narrowing of achievement gaps since NCLB was enacted. For example, results from the 2005 NAEP show more progress was made by nine-year-olds in reading from 2000 to 2005 than in the previous 28 years combined. NCLB has certainly not "fixed" public education, nor has it closed the achievement gap; but tangible improvements have resulted from this legislation, and they provide critical information we can use to strengthen the next reauthorization.

Moreover, despite assertions to the contrary, these results have not come about due to more students dropping out of school. While national graduation rates are unacceptably low, a 2009 study conducted by the America's Promise Alliance found that graduation rates actually inched up in recent years, from 66 percent in 1995 to 71 percent in 2005. The rate still falls far short of acceptable, and it is not a huge increase, but it is a significant one—certainly not the decline some have falsely claimed. . . .

Improving Local Accountability

In a seminal study in Chicago, researchers found that in classrooms in which teachers employed "authentic instruction"—i.e., a focus on the full body of skills needed to master a subject—score gains on the Illinois Test of Basic Skills (ITBS) exceeded the national average by 20 percent. Conversely, in classes in which students were given few authentic assignments—i.e., in which there was a narrow, drill and kill approach— ITBS gains were much less than the national average. Moreover, the type of instruction offered was found to be a function of "teacher disposition and choices" rather than the particular characteristics or achievement levels of the students being taught.

In a comprehensive review of the "teaching to the test" issue, Craig Jerald concludes: "Accountability and standardized tests need not be in conflict with good instruction. . . . Teaching to the test by dumbing down instruction offers only a kind of fool's gold, promising a payoff that does not deliver. The choice between good instruction and good test scores is a false one."

EVALUATING THE AUTHOR'S ARGUMENTS:

The author of the viewpoint you have just read has written that the issue brief from which the viewpoint is taken is intended for a wide readership made up of "policy makers, advocates, parents, educators, and the general public." Identify ideas, language, and evidence that you believe would be particularly effective for reaching an audience of policy makers and educators; do the same for an audience of parents and the general public.

Standardized Testing Has Harmed Poor and Minority Students

Monty Neill

"Large numbers of students of color, low-income students, and immigrant students feel that their futures are being destroyed by a test."

In the following viewpoint, education researcher and advocate Monty Neill describes the ways in which high-stakes educational testing is particularly damaging to students in low-income communities. Students in these communities are made to take the same tests as their wealthier peers, he explains, but they are not given the same quality of preparation for the tests. The resulting low scores and the emphasis placed on scores, he argues, make it more difficult for these students to succeed in college and careers.

Neill is executive director of the National Center for Fair and Open Testing and chair of the Forum on Educational Accountability. He has studied and written about testing in the public schools since 1987.

Monty Neill, "A Child Is Not a Test Score: Assessment as a Civil Rights Issue," *Root & Branch*, vol. 2, Fall 2009, pp. 28, 30–31, 35. Reproduced by permission.

AS YOU READ, CONSIDER THE FOLLOWING QUESTIONS:
1. Which subjects and activities might districts in poorer communities eliminate to create more time for test preparation, according to the author?
2. Was the passage of No Child Left Behind a Democratic or a Republican effort, as reported by Neill?
3. Why, according to the author, do some teachers no longer teach writing and research skills?

"The function of education is to teach one to think intensively and to think critically. Intelligence plus character—that is the goal of true education."—Martin Luther King, Jr.

Across the country, students have exposed the damaging educational consequences of high-stakes standardized tests. They have decried being denied a diploma because of a test score and exposed the way incessant test preparation deforms curriculum, instruction and learning.

Macario Guajardo, a 16-year-old from south Texas who for years boycotted the state's standardized test, the Texas Assessment of Knowledge and Skills (TAKS), explained to a state legislative committee on education reform the consequences for learning: "When I was in elementary, schools were basically like a TAKS factory, and students were almost like little robots. I don't remember there being any room for serious, creative and critical thinkers."

Carolyn, also aged 16, wrote in the California *Bee*, a daily newspaper, "District tests, including the high school exit exam, should be eliminated since there is no educational point to them. . . . Too much classroom time is wasted on test preparation and taking tests. That time should be spent on actual learning of subjects, not on the steps of how to eliminate answers" (i.e. incorrect options on multiple choice questions). She added, "The focus of our education system should not be based on tests, but on the individual needs of students." . . .

Unequal Education

Districts in poorer communities, especially communities of color that have fewer qualified teachers and inadequate books, laboratories and libraries, are expected to perform at the same levels as districts that have far more financial and educational resources. The inequity is compounded when districts gut art, music classes and sports for the rote memorization, constant quizzing and testing that limit time for creative and analytical thinking. Wealthier districts, whose students are better prepared for these tests, devote far less time to test preparation and don't suffer the impact of narrowed curricula.

A Californians for Justice report explained, "Any conversation with high school students from around the state reveals that students are

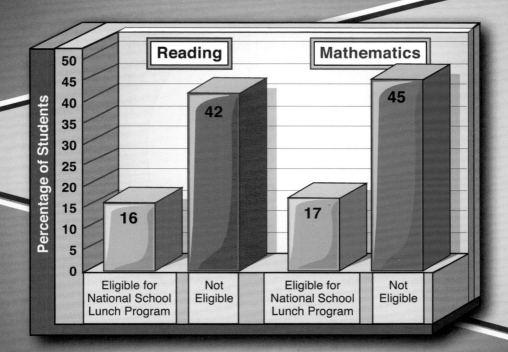

Percent of Students Scoring at or Above Proficient on the NAEP Test in 2009

Eighth graders who were eligible for the National School Lunch Program, a measure of low-income status, performed less well than their peers who were not eligible for the program on the 2009 National Assessment of Education Progress.

Taken from: *The Nation's Report Card, 2009.* U.S. Department of Education.

extremely demoralized by the exit exam. It is clear that large numbers of students of color, low-income students, and immigrant students feel that their futures are being destroyed by a test for which they have not been prepared."

As Boston student Gregory pointed out, "They are just training us for the workforce . . . trying to train you to sit in one place and do simple operations for eight hours." Caroline added, "You always have a lot of people saying that you kids are the future. But how can we be the future if we are not getting what we need?"

The stories of educational damage occur and recur because high-stakes standardized testing has come to dominate learning and class time. Tests are widely used as a sole hurdle for student grade promotion, graduation, or program placement, and they control opportunities, curriculum and instruction in the name of accountability.

The interaction of under-resourced schools and testing most powerfully hits students of color. They are disproportionately denied diplomas or grade promotion, and the schools they attend are the ones most likely to fare poorly on the tests and face sanctions such as restructuring. . . .

School Reform Made Things Worse

Test-based "school reform" such as NCLB [No Child Left Behind], which passed with support from both Democrats and Republicans, is an effort to improve results while ignoring the existence of the education debt.

The tools used to improve results—tests and sanctions—actually make things worse. Low-income students, who are disproportionately children of color, go to under-resourced schools that serve up a thin gruel of test preparation. So long as such a system remains in place, the pipeline to college and good jobs for low-income and minority-group youths will remain narrow, but the pipelines to prison and unemployment will remain wide.

High-stakes testing undermines school quality. What is it about the use of standardized tests as the primary, even sole arbiter of school quality that is problematic? Partly it is because, in the face of escalating sanctions, some schools and districts have taken harmful actions such as increasing suspensions and expulsions of low scorers—removing perceived problem kids from the classrooms instead of dealing with their problems. And partly it is the damage done to teaching.

"Apartheid Education"

Testing's control over teaching is unevenly applied. The drill-and-kill school practices that guarantee students will not be ready for college, skilled employment, lifelong learning or effective citizenship are most prevalent in schools serving low-income children of color. No one has documented this more powerfully than Jonathan Kozol in *Shame of the Nation*. Building on his earlier exposé, *Savage Inequalities*, of the vastly unequal opportunities provided in different communities across the nation, Kozol describes in painful detail the brain-deadening, emotionally stultifying consequences of scripted curricula and test preparation in what he terms "apartheid education."

Suburban middle- and upper-class schools succumb to a degree to teaching to state exams, but teaching to the test is nowhere near as prevalent or powerful in those communities. And the suburban schools certainly do not employ the tightly scripted curricula widely used in urban schools.

Critics of the No Child Left Behind Act argue that poorer school districts have fewer resources than more affluent school districts but are expected to perform at the same level.

The learning gaps revealed by standardized tests mask worse gaps in more advanced learning skills. For example, students in well-to-do schools typically learn to write research papers, which colleges expect students to do. There are no research papers on standardized tests. If the primary goal is to boost test scores . . . teachers will not take time out to teach needed research and writing skills. As noted psychologist Robert Sternberg wrote, "The increasingly massive and far-reaching use of conventional standardized tests is one of the most effective, if unintentional, vehicles this country has created for suppressing creativity." That suppression, too, most powerfully affects students who are most subject to the tests. . . .

FAST FACT

More than 60 percent of black and Hispanic students attend high-poverty schools, compared with 30 percent of Asian and 18 percent of white students, according to Harvard University's Civil Rights Project.

Setting Priorities

What do we as a nation want to prioritize? Spurious and illusory steps toward equity through standardization, or real improvement efforts in which high-quality assessment is one essential part.

More significantly, how much less should low-income communities and communities of color and their advocates settle for? We might agree that it is pie in the sky to think that all kids will be in schools that spend $25,000 per pupil each year, as many elite private schools do, or spend in the upper teens per pupil as many wealthy suburban schools do. But, are no art classes or science labs acceptable? Is no consideration of the whole child and her or his relationship to actual communities okay? We might indeed prioritize reading, writing and math, but all of those skills can and should be integrated into richer opportunities—and assessments and accountability need to take those broader needs into account.

To settle for less is not only to settle for obvious inequality, it is to consign the children of the poor to perpetually less—to not give them the educational opportunities they need to succeed in higher education, at work and as effective citizens. Settling for less means leaving them behind while pretending to enable them to catch up. Dr. King's epigram that opens this article clearly does not support the emphasis on rote learning of "basics" or drills for filling in the bubbles on multiple-choice tests.

The answers to these questions will depend on activism by parents, students, educators, communities, and organizations. Without a concerted push for change, our nation is all too likely to continue undermining education for our most vulnerable youth.

EVALUATING THE AUTHORS' ARGUMENTS:

This and the preceding viewpoint both address high school graduation rates. The Education Equality Project argues that too many low-income and minority students are being allowed to graduate without having learned enough to be ready for college or the workplace. Monty Neill worries that too many students are being denied high school diplomas because of poor performances on tests. After reading both viewpoints, how do you think this issue could be resolved?

Standardized Testing Is Improving Education for Disabled Students

Advocacy Institute

"With these requirements [to pass standardized tests] have come . . . accommodation policies that make it possible for students with disabilities to demonstrate what they have learned."

The following viewpoint by the Advocacy Institute addresses the improvements that the 2001 No Child Left Behind Act brought to children with disabilities. Before passage of the law, the author argues, it was easy for districts to ignore the special needs of students with disabilities, because the districts did not have to prove that they were teaching these students well. The author concludes that with the law's passage and its requirement that all students pass the same standardized tests, school districts were required to provide special education students with qualified teachers and a challenging curriculum to help them meet the same academic standards as their peers. The Advocacy Institute is a nonprofit organization that works to improve the lives of people with disabilities.

Advocacy Institute, "7 Million Students with Disabilities Need No Child Left Behind," March 2007. Reproduced by permission.

For too long this nation's students with disabilities have been overlooked, undertaught, and left out. The No Child Left Behind Act of 2001 [NCLB] shone a bright light on the persistent underachievement of important subgroups of students and only then did educators begin to focus long needed attention on achievement of students with identified disabilities.

No Child Left Behind has finally brought students with disabilities into state and district-wide assessments. Despite a requirement added to the Individuals with Disabilities Education Act (IDEA) in the 1997 amendments requiring all students with disabilities to be included in state and district-wide assessments, it was not until the passage of NCLB that schools, school districts, and states finally began to include all students in the state's accountability system, to teach them what they have a right to learn and to report their performance.

With these requirements have come the development of accommodation policies that make it possible for students with disabilities to demonstrate what they have learned as well as alternate assessments based on alternate standards for those few students with cognitive disabilities that preclude them from attaining grade-level standards. Still, we have miles to go in developing universally designed tests, appropriate alternate assessments, and technically sound, well-administered testing accommodations for those students with disabilities who need them.

Demanding Accountability

No Child Left Behind has made schools accountable for ensuring that students with disabilities have access to a challenging curriculum. For at least 10 years IDEA has required all eligible students to be provided an individualized education program (IEP) designed to meet their instructional needs and enable them to make progress in the general education curriculum. Yet, not until NCLB required schools and school districts to disaggregate the performance of students with disabilities did access to the same challenging academic content begin to become a reality. Still, challenges remain, particularly the unacceptably high percentage of schools that are allowed to escape publicly reporting the performance of students with disabilities. . . .

A Better Education

No Child Left Behind has addressed the lack of highly qualified teachers. Despite years of federal investments in research on effective instructional practices, teacher recruitment, pre-service and in-service training,

The No Child Left Behind Act requires school districts to provide special education students with qualified teachers to help them meet the same academic standards as nondisabled children.

and assistive technology, not until the NCLB requirements for highly qualified teachers were amendments providing for highly qualified special education teachers added to IDEA 2004, ensuring that students with disabilities would receive instruction from both regular and special educators who have academic content knowledge in the field they are teaching. Still, for the achievement gap to be narrowed, much remains to be accomplished in promoting higher expectations for students with disabilities and implementing evidence-based teaching and instructional practices through effective and ongoing professional development.

- Roughly 10 percent of special education positions nationally— 39,140 positions—are filled by uncertified personnel who serve approximately 600,000 students with disabilities.

Source: SPeNSE, Study of Personnel Needs in Special Education 2002

- Only 57 percent of special education teachers say they are "very" familiar with their state's academic content for the subjects they teach.

Source: Quality Counts 2004: Count Me In, Education Week 2004

Data reported during the past five years [2003–2007] indicates that students with disabilities were left behind or not considered in the effort to raise standards and improve instruction in our nation's public schools:

- Nearly 38 percent of students with disabilities ages 14 and older dropped out of school during the 2001–2002 school year. Only 51 percent graduated with a standard diploma in the same year.
- Only 35 states and the District of Columbia require schools or district report cards to include information separately on the test participation rates and performance of students with disabilities, Few states—seven and 15 respectively—require schools or districts to report dropout and graduation rates separately for students in special education.
- Grades given to secondary school students with disabilities have been found to have no correlation to real academic functioning, misleading parents about how their child is actually performing.

Low Expectations

Even with the passage of No Child Left Behind and corresponding amendments to the Individuals with Disabilities Education Act in

2004, children with disabilities are most certainly left behind and affected by the lack of expectations they face in their schools:

- Only one-fifth of teachers think that "all" or "most" of their special education students can score at the proficient level on state exams.
- The vast majority, 86 percent, of teachers feel that it is "unfair" to evaluate special education students on how well they master academic content standards based on test scores. Eighty-nine percent feel it is unfair to teachers to be evaluated on how well IEP students score on state tests.
- Only seven states require that the IEPs of students with disabilities address state academic content standards.

Under NCLB's "accountability" provisions, school districts and individual schools must make what the Act terms "adequate yearly progress" (AYP) towards ensuring that all students achieve at least a "proficient" level on state assessments in reading and math by the 2014–2015 school year. Each state sets the standard for what constitutes "proficient," and defines "adequate yearly progress," per certain requirements set out in NCLB and approved by the U.S. Department of Education. To exclude students with disabilities from being included in the determination of AYP as required by NCLB, or to marginalize their participation by alternate measures, would constitute a violation of their civil rights under Section 504 of the Rehabilitation Act.

FAST FACT

The National Institute of Mental Health has estimated that there are approximately 4 million schoolchildren with learning disabilities in the United States.

Children with disabilities, including those students with significant disabilities, are making progress under No Child Left Behind. The challenge for these children, their families, and the advocates who are allied with them will be to ensure that our nation's education leaders view the education of students with disabilities to high academic standards as an opportunity and a shared goal. As Congress prepares to examine and reauthorize NCLB, it is encouraged to stay the course on accountability for students with disabilities.

High-Stakes Testing Can Create Obstacles for Disabled Students

Candace Cortiella

> *"Standardized testing can . . . pose serious obstacles and consequences [for disabled students]."*

In the following viewpoint, Candace Cortiella warns that reliance on so-called high-stakes testing, such as tests that students must pass in order to earn a high school diploma, can be harmful to students with disabilities. These students struggle with the tests, she contends, and their failure to do well on them can lead to their being held back a grade or dropping out of school. Schools must do more to make sure students with disabilities are prepared for the tests, given reasonable accommodations to help them take the tests, and provided with opportunities to keep working on skills that they have not yet mastered. Cortiella is an advocate and consultant for families of children with disabilities.

Candace Cortiella, "Implications of High-Stakes Testing for Students with Learning Disabilities," *GreatSchools*, January, 2010. Reproduced by permission.

AS YOU READ, CONSIDER THE FOLLOWING QUESTIONS:
  1. As reported by Cortiella, how many students with disabilities are made to repeat a grade, i.e., are "retained"?
  2. Approximately what percentage of students in the general population drop out before graduating high school, according to the author?
  3. Why should remediation, or extra work to make up for weaknesses, not focus on test-taking skills, according to Cortiella?

Over the past decade, states have been engaged in a variety of education reform efforts designed to improve the quality of public education. One highly visible reform is "high-stakes" testing. The purpose of such tests is to improve student achievement. While students with learning disabilities have a lot to gain from increased focus on student achievement, high-stakes standardized testing can also pose serious obstacles and consequences. This article examines the current state of high-stakes testing and its implications for students with learning disabilities (LD). . . .

Q: *What are some of the most significant risks posed by high-stakes tests for students with learning disabilities?*

A: Some of the most significant risks include:

Increased Grade Retention

We know that large performance gaps exist between students with disabilities and their non-disabled peers. We also know that students with disabilities continue to be retained much more often than the general population—more than one-third are retained at grade level at least once, usually in elementary school. Promotion tests—the fastest growing area of high-stakes testing—will most likely contribute to even more retention of students with learning disabilities, despite the fact that retention has been shown to be an ineffective intervention to improving academic achievement. More importantly, students who are retained are much more likely to drop out later in school, and those retained more than once are *dramatically* more likely to drop out. Research on retention shows that grade repeaters as adults are more likely to be unemployed, living on public assistance, or in prison than adults who did not repeat a grade.

Increased Possibility of Dropping Out

Data show that students with disabilities fail large-scale tests at higher rates than other students, especially in the years immediately following the introduction of such tests. One important reason for this is their lack of access to the curriculum on which the tests are based. Failing a high-stakes test, such as a test required for graduation with a standard diploma, can increase the likelihood that low achievers will drop out of school. We already know that nearly 30 percent of students with learning disabilities drop out of school (compared to 11% of the general student population), and we know that dropping out of school is associated with poor life outcomes in regard to postsecondary education and employment. . . .

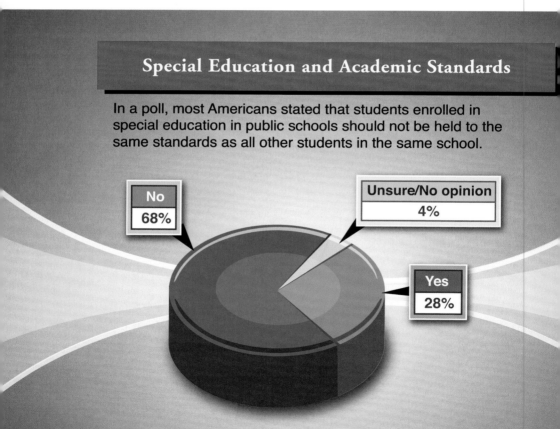

Special Education and Academic Standards

In a poll, most Americans stated that students enrolled in special education in public schools should not be held to the same standards as all other students in the same school.

No
68%

Unsure/No opinion
4%

Yes
28%

Taken from: Phi Delta Kappa/Gallup survey, November 15, 2005.

Awarding of Alternative High School Diplomas or Certificates

To compensate students with disabilities who fail high school graduation tests, many states are developing one or more alternative diplomas and certificates. These include nonstandard diplomas such as IEP [individual educational program] diplomas, certificates of completion, certificates of attendance, and modified diplomas. There is little research on the value of such alternative diplomas and certificates. Many may not be accepted by colleges and universities. Meanwhile, the existence of such alternatives provides the opportunity for students with learning disabilities to be "tracked" into high school course work that will not provide the necessary credits for a standard diploma, nor provide the student access to the subject matter of graduation tests. Parents need to be well informed regarding the implications of any nonstandard diplomas and should be sure that they are involved in decisions regarding the high school diploma track of their student with LD.

Q: *What are the barriers to success on high-stakes tests for students with LD?*

A: The greatest barriers include:

Inadequate Opportunity to Learn

Undoubtedly the largest barrier to success is the lack of exposure to the subject matter and skills tested by large-scale assessments. While every state is required to have high academic standards that are the same for every student, we know that many students with disabilities are not yet being taught to those standards. In fact, in a recent survey only 57 percent of special education teachers said they are "very" familiar with their

Two students graduate from a school for special education students. Many states are developing alternative diplomas and certificates for disabled and special education students.

state's academic content for the subjects they teach. The survey also found that only seven states require that the IEPs of students with disabilities address state content standards. Yet another study found that it does not appear that IEP teams "ensure that the curriculum and instruction received by the student through the individual education program (IEP) is aligned with test content and that the student has had adequate opportunity to learn the material covered by the test."

More Restrictive Placements

Research on state accountability systems indicates that states with high school graduation tests tend to place students with disabilities in more restrictive settings. The opportunity to learn the subject matter and skills that are aligned to state- and district-wide assessments can be further compromised when students are placed in more restrictive classroom settings, where they will invariably have less access to both the general curriculum and to the general education teachers who are most qualified to teach that curriculum.

Lack of Reasonable Accommodations

Federal laws require that students with learning disabilities be provided reasonable accommodations and auxiliary aids and services in order to participate fully in state- and district-wide assessment programs. The National Center on Educational Outcomes (NCEO) says this about accommodations: "Accommodations are changes in testing materials or procedures that enable students to participate in assessments in a way that allows abilities to be assessed rather than disabilities. They are provided to 'level the playing field.' Without accommodations, the assessment may not accurately measure the student's knowledge and skills." . . .

Inadequate Access to Remediation

Students who do not pass a high-stakes test should be provided meaningful opportunities for remediation. According to one recent study, the economic costs of helping students with disabilities pass exit exams are typically underestimated and overlooked. Remediation should be targeted to the knowledge and skill deficit reflected in the test performance, not merely on test-taking techniques, since it is well known that scores on a test can increase as students become familiar with the test format without any real improvement in mastery of the subject matter. Students should have adequate opportunities to retake tests once remediation has occurred.

Over-Reliance on a Single Test Score

There is no single measure that can accurately reflect the knowledge and skills of a student. Moreover, students with disabilities perform more poorly on standardized tests than their non-disabled peers, so over-reliance on such test scores has a disproportionately negative impact on students with LD, as well as minority students. While there is evidence that course grades frequently have little correlation to real academic performance, a variety of measures need to be considered when making high-stakes decisions. The testing profession's Joint Standards state that "in elementary and secondary education, a decision or characterization that will have a major impact on a test taker should not automatically be made on the basis of a single test score."

EVALUATING THE AUTHORS' ARGUMENTS:

This and the previous viewpoint both deal with the needs of students with disabilities and the degrees to which these needs have been addressed by the No Child Left Behind Act of 2001. The first viewpoint, from the Advocacy Institute, focuses on how the act's requirement that students be tested has forced schools to pay more attention to educating students with disabilities. The second viewpoint, by Candace Cortiella, argues that the tests are not fair to students with disabilities. Can both viewpoints be right? How can policy makers use what seem to be opposing viewpoints to find the answers to complicated questions?

Chapter 2

Are Standardized Tests Beneficial to Teachers?

Much controversy has arisen over the methods and procedures for evaluating students.

Good Teachers "Teach to the Test"

Walt Gardner

"If we're being honest, teaching to the test is done by almost all . . . effective teachers."

In the following viewpoint, educator Walt Gardner claims proudly that when he was a teacher he taught to the test. It is important, he argues, for teachers to prepare students for the particular skills and areas of knowledge that standardized tests will examine. To spend significant class time on material that will not prepare students for the tests, he contends, is irresponsible. Teachers have many demands on their time and attention, he concludes, and the best way to balance priorities is to focus on what will be tested. Gardner, a former longtime high school English teacher and school of education lecturer, writes an education blog called *Reality Check* for Education Week.

AS YOU READ, CONSIDER THE FOLLOWING QUESTIONS:
1. According to the author, what important distinction do people often fail to make when they discuss "teaching to the test"?
2. In what ways are the roles of a teacher like those of an athletic coach, as described by Gardner?
3. Why, in the author's opinion, is covering "as much material as possible" a poor way to structure a school curriculum?

I have a confession to make. For the entire 28 years that I taught high school English, I taught to the test. And I'm proud to finally admit it.

I know that 'fessing up to this perceived transgression will reflexively draw clamor from everyone with children in school. That's because teaching to the test is considered tantamount to cheating on your income tax returns. But stay with me here: This type of reaction is the result of a fundamental misunderstanding of both curriculum and instruction.

If we're being honest, teaching to the test is done by almost all other effective teachers. In fact, I did so—along with many other an effective educator—way before teachers were evaluated on the basis of their students' ability to perform on the standardized tests that now constitute the sine qua non [essential element] of accountability.

That's because it is eminently sound pedagogy [the art of teaching].

An Important Distinction

There is a distinct difference between teaching to the broad body of skills and knowledge that a test represents (good), and teaching to the exact items that will appear on the standardized test (indefensible and illegal). Teaching students how to answer a particular set of items that appears on a test shortchanges them ethically and educationally. The confusing part arises when we fail to make that distinction.

Let me be more concrete. If one of the goals of an English course is for students to gain the ability to write a persuasive essay that contains a thesis statement supported by evidence, then it behooves the teacher to provide students with practice writing persuasive essays that contain both.

In the past many teachers have "taught to the test" by preparing students to know only the material they will be tested on in the standardized tests. Teachers in the Denver school system shown here can earn merit pay increases in various ways including better test scores or teaching at a difficult school.

Practice is accompanied by critique from the teacher. It's the feedback from the teacher that lets students know if they're on the right track to mastering the required skills.

Technically, this is teaching to the test, but because students do not know beforehand what question they will ultimately be asked, it is instructionally defensible, helpful, and educational. In fact, it would be irresponsible for a teacher to provide students with practice writing descriptive or narrative essays that *aren't* the type to be tested. It's not that such writing is wrong or harmful. On the contrary, both have their places in English classes. But giving students such writing practice does not help them master the skills to write persuasive essays—the types of essays that are on the test.

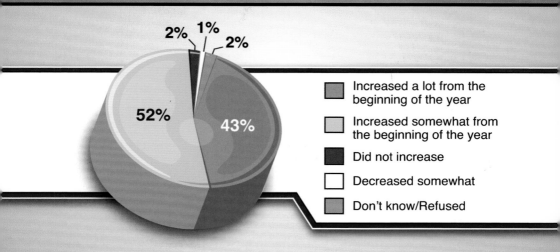

Teaching What Is Tested

In 2009, 890 teachers were asked to complete this sentence: "This year, as a result of my instruction, the subject matter test scores of most of my students. . . . " Most teachers believed that they had taught their students the material covered by standardized tests.

2% 1% 2%

52%

43%

- Increased a lot from the beginning of the year
- Increased somewhat from the beginning of the year
- Did not increase
- Decreased somewhat
- Don't know/Refused

Taken from: Public Agenda and Learning Point Associates, *Teaching for a Living: How Teachers See the Profession Today*, October 2009.

Teachers and Coaches

In sports, coaches have long "coached to the game." They identify the best way of transferring practice onto the game field. They design routines and scrimmages that mimic as closely as possible what will ultimately be required in a particular game.

If track coaches want a team member to run the 100-meter dash, for example, they don't have them run a 10K. There may be some overlap, but it is not enough to justify the time and effort involved to spend a good chunk of practice working on it.

Again, that's different from coaches fixing the game or the race.

The distinction is crucial in today's debate over the method used to identify effective teachers because it also calls into question another widely misunderstood concept—the curriculum.

In an attempt to help schools provide a quality education, reformers mistakenly believe that covering as much material as possible is the way to go. But this approach is counterproductive. It overloads teachers by designing a curriculum that emphasizes breadth over depth.

The result is that teachers are given far too many targets to aim at in their lessons. These extensive lists of high-blown objectives certainly look impressive on paper, but they cannot realistically be addressed by teachers in their day-to-day instructional decisions. This is particularly the case when classes are composed of students with a wide range of individual differences. And this doesn't even take into consideration the time constraints of a given school year, which puts great pressure on teachers in planning their lessons.

In light of the demands of the accountability movement, teaching to the test is an issue that needs to be fully understood.

So the next time you hear that your child's teacher is "teaching to the test," think about this: The teacher may well be engaging in perfectly solid instruction.

> # FAST FACT
>
> According to the founders of BASIS charter school in Tucson, Arizona, it was ranked the best high school in the country by *Newsweek* magazine in 2008. Much of their success comes from "teaching to the test"—the Advanced Placement tests in eight subjects.

As you may notice as you read through this book, terms including "teaching to the test" mean different things to different people, and it sometimes happens that people who seem to disagree about a practice or a policy are actually disagreeing about what a term means. How does Walt Gardner help clarify his points, and make his argument stronger, by carefully defining "teaching to the test" as he will use it in his essay? How closely does his definition match others you have encountered? Give two examples.

Teaching to the Test Weakens Education

Judy Willis

> "The toxic NCLB pressure resulted in teach-to-the-test curriculum with its drill-and-kill worksheets and memorization."

In the following viewpoint, Judy Willis maintains that the teaching to the test that has followed the institution of No Child Left Behind has resulted in teaching that focuses on rote memorization of facts/ideas without context or relevance. Such teaching does not provide the cues for novelty or pleasure that the brain looks for and that attract its attention. As a result, students lose interest and become bored, and their brains look for alternate sources of stimulation. The toxic effect of this teaching/learning environment is made worse by the stress that accompanies standardized testing. This toxic environment needs to be replaced by education that is relevant to students' lives, interests, and experiences without being intimidating.

Willis is a board-certified neurologist and middle school teacher who is an authority on classroom strategies derived from brain research.

AS YOU READ, CONSIDER THE FOLLOWING QUESTIONS:
  1. Through what does the brain learn and to what does it give priority, according to Willis?
  2. Why do teachers teach to the test rather than encourage children's critical thinking skills, according to the author?
  3. What does brain research show happens when the brain has positive motivation to learn, according to Willis?

Children are naturally curious and have magnificent senses of wonder. They want to learn and explore. Often starting at age three or four, especially if they have older siblings, children look forward with great excitement to the day they can start school. The big day comes and things might go well for a few years. Then something changes and school is no longer a wondrous place. How sad that is.

The No Child Left Behind agenda has resulted in one-size-fits-all cookbook curriculum that leaves little room for teachers to make lessons engaging enough to be considered "valuable" by the brain's intake filters. All learning comes through the senses and what sensory information comes in is the unconscious decision of our primitive lower brains. Priority is given to HERE-ME-NOW input such as novelty or input that previously was associated with pleasure.

Animals need that sorting system to be alert to signs of danger or potential pleasure (the sight of potential prey or the smell of a potential mate). Through natural selection, the animals with brain intake filters most successful at alerting to novelty and change, have survived. Humans have this same primitive brain information intake system. At the unconscious, reflexive level our brains are programmed to let in input (pay attention to) novelty, change, and cues that are linked with pleasure.

Those prerequisites to paying attention are not found in classrooms where the teacher lectures and the students "memorize" facts they regurgitate on tests and soon forget. Neuroimaging PET and fMRI scans provide evidence that this type of rote learning is the most quickly forgotten because the information is never stored in long-term memory storage. As students lose interest in lecture-and-memorize classes,

With Secretary of Education Arne Duncan behind him, President Barack Obama delivers remarks on the Race to the Top program and says he does not believe standardized testing is a benefit to students.

their attention wanders and disruptive behaviors are the natural consequence. Even for children who are able to maintain focus on rote instruction, the disruptive responses of their classmates are encroaching more and more on their teachers' instruction time as teachers spend more time trying to maintain order.

Today's brain toxic focus of fact memorization is not the fault of teachers, many of whom started teaching before NCLB invaded their classrooms. In those days, in the best classrooms, lessons were interactive and information was delivered through activities, projects, field trips, discovery, and class visits by professionals who used the math, science, or language in their cool jobs or hobbies.

The toxic NCLB pressure resulted in teach-to-the-test curriculum with its drill-and-kill worksheets and memorization. The cost to our children is the loss of the golden opportunity to build on their curiosity and enthusiasm. As early as kindergarten children begin to begrudge their time in school and gradually their brains construct neural circuits for self-stimulation (talking during lectures, drawing pictures instead of doing boring worksheets, fidgeting with change in their pockets or toys hidden in their desks). I'll save for another time the fact that the toxicity of the stress of boredom and frustration also causes the sustained release of too much cortisol, which kills neurons and damages the immune system. . . .

> # FAST FACT
>
> In a survey conducted by *Education Week*, 66 percent of teachers thought that state tests were forcing them to concentrate too much on what was tested, leaving other important subjects uncovered.

Parents' intervention is now needed to help children reach their highest potentials and find ways to help them connect to the information in mind-numbing classes. Parents can use the brain-friendly practices used in great classrooms by teachers who know how the brain learns. These strategies will breathe life and increase unconscious attentiveness to the mandated, overstuffed curriculum. Without parent stimulation, children's brain pathways to the prefrontal cortex (highest thinking conscious decision making brain) are pruned away from disuse.

If we give children experiences that make the classroom lessons relevant, we are counteracting the toxic classroom experiences. When children are prepared with background knowledge that helps them personally relate to school units, new information will reach the prefrontal cortex, the reflective, thinking, conscious brain where creativity, prediction, deduction, independent judgment, memory building, and insight await the arrival of new input to process.

Many schools are cutting back on the extracurricular activities that build character and add multidimensionality to learning. Those children are feeling more disconnected from their teachers and schools, but parents can use art, music, family field trips, and meaningful discussion to increase children's connection to their school subjects.

Budgets and job security in the school system are tied to schools' abilities to mass-produce students trained to pass standardized tests that reward rote memorization skills. Instead of encouraging children's critical thinking skills, teachers are pushed to "teach to the test" and students in their classrooms are losing interest in the information force fed to them in these toxic classrooms. With home supplementary engagement of children's personal connections, background knowledge, and curiosity parents can bring life back into their learning while helping children build the critical thinking and reasoning skills that are being sacrificed with this rote memorization approach to teaching.

Learning can be a joy. Parents know their children better than any teacher ever will. Using the growing field of evidence-based neuroscience and learning research strategies now available, parents can assist their children learn what they need to know to pass the tests and much, MUCH more. Using strategies that engage and captivate your children's interests, parents can work with them at home to enhance their personal connection with and critical thinking about the dry, factual data they are served up at school.

The realities of standardized tests and increasingly structured, if not synchronized, curriculum continue to build the levels of classroom toxic stress for children. Cutting edge neuroimaging research (PET scans, fMRI scans) reveals significant disturbances in the brain's learning circuits and the brain's chemical messengers that accompany stressful learning environments. Science has provided us with information about the negative brain impact of stress and anxiety and the beneficial changes in the brain that are seen when children are motivated by and personally connected to their lessons.

In the past decade, the neuroimaging and brain-mapping research that I evaluated from my perspective as a neurologist and classroom teacher have provided objective support to the student-centered educational model where students feel they are partners in their education. This brain research demonstrates that superior learning takes place when information is presented in ways relevant to students' lives, interests, and experiences. Lessons must be stimulating and challenging, without being intimidating, for the increasing curriculum standards to be achieved without stress, anxiety, boredom, and alienation becoming the emotions children experience in their classrooms.

During the fifteen years I practiced adult and child neurology with neuroimaging and brain mapping as part of my diagnostic tool kit, I worked with patients of all ages with disorders of brain function, including learning differences. When I returned to university to obtain my teaching credential and Masters of Education degree, these neuroimaging tools that I had used as in my neurology practice had become available to researchers in the field of education.

This brain research demonstrates that superior learning takes place when classroom experiences are motivating and engaging. Positive motivation impacts brain metabolism, conduction of nerve impulses through the memory areas, and the release of neurotransmitters (brain chemicals like dopamine) that increase attention, focus, organization of thoughts, and high-level thinking called executive function. We now see the brain response when lessons are relevant to children's lives, interests, and experiences so each child feels he or she is a partner in the learning process and develops personally relevant goals that motivate attentive focus to the topics of study.

EVALUATING THE AUTHORS' ARGUMENTS:

Compare this viewpoint by Judy Willis with the preceding one by Walt Gardner, who argues that teaching to the test is a good educational practice. Are they talking about the same thing? Are there any points they might agree on? Support your answer with evidence from each viewpoint.

Teachers Should Be Evaluated According to Their Students' Test Scores

Arne Duncan

"To somehow suggest that we should not link student achievement and teacher effectiveness is like suggesting we judge a sports team without looking at the box score."

The following viewpoint was originally a speech by U.S. secretary of education Arne Duncan, delivered at an Institute of Education Sciences Research Conference. In the viewpoint Duncan explains the importance of collecting and interpreting data as part of the effort to improve education. Teachers must not resist using data—typically gathered from standardized test scores—to help determine which students are learning and which teachers are teaching well, he argues. More school districts, he concludes, should make use of data to monitor student progress and to understand how teachers succeed.

Arne Duncan, "Robust Data Gives Us the Roadmap to Reform," U.S. Department of Education, June 8, 2009.

There's a lot I don't like about *No Child Left Behind* (*NCLB*),
but I will always give it credit for exposing our nation's dread-
ful achievement gaps. It changed American education forever
and forced us to take responsibility for every single child, regardless
of race, background, or ability. And this is just one example of how
data affects policy and there are many, many more. . . .

In the months and years ahead, we will ask thousands of communities across America to close and reopen schools based on data showing that they are underperforming. That has never happened before
and it will be as difficult as it is important. It will change and improve
the life chances of children from underserved communities forever.

We will ask millions of teachers to use student achievement and
annual growth to drive instruction and evaluation. Parents need to
understand that. We ask elected officials in states across America to
embrace higher standards even though the initial data for their states
may reflect badly on them and their schools. This will take real political courage with short-term pain leading to long-term gain.

Clearly, this is a lot to ask of people. It is our responsibility to make
this experience as safe and comfortable for people as possible. People
need to get it and they need to be part of the cause of public education. And that means they need to understand data.

Data Does Not Lie

Data may not tell us the whole truth, but it certainly doesn't lie. So
what is the data telling us today? It tells us that something like 30
percent of our children, our students, are not finishing high school.
It tells us that many adults who do graduate go on to college but need

remedial education. They're receiving high school diplomas, but they are not ready for college. . . .

Our best teachers today are using real-time data in ways that would have been unimaginable just five years ago [2004].

They need to know how well their students are performing. They want to know exactly what they need to do to teach and how to teach. It makes their job easier and ultimately much more rewarding. They aren't guessing or talking in generalities anymore. They feel as if they're starting to crack the code.

We will also ask whether the data around student achievement is linked to teacher effectiveness. Believe it or not, several states, including New York, Wisconsin, and California, have laws that create a firewall between students and teacher data. Think about that: Laws that prohibit us from connecting children to the adults who teach them.

Usually, firewalls are set up for our protection. They prevent hackers from getting into our computers and they block our children from visiting inappropriate Web sites. But these state firewalls don't help us. They hurt all of us. They impede our ability to serve students and better understand how we can improve American education.

U.S. secretary of education Arne Duncan has done a nationwide Courage in the Classroom tour to discuss standardized testing and educational reform with educators across the country.

Linking Student Achievement to Teacher Effectiveness

I brought this up in a meeting in California [in May 2009] and a local union leader said the following: "Gather data so you can decide who the good teachers are? Wrong. We need more data, but not to use it as a basis for teachers' pay."

Now I absolutely respect the concerns of teachers that test scores alone should never be used solely to determine salaries. I absolutely agree with that sentiment. I also appreciate that growth models as they exist today are far less than perfect. We have a lot of work still ahead of us.

But to somehow suggest that we should not link student achievement and teacher effectiveness is like suggesting we judge a sports team without looking at the box score.

It's like saying, since standardized tests are not perfect, eliminate testing until they are. I think that's simply ridiculous. We need to monitor progress. We need to know what is and is not working and why.

In California, they have 300,000 teachers. If you took the top 10 percent, they have 30,000 of the best teachers in the world. If you took the bottom 10 percent, they have 30,000 teachers that should probably find another profession, yet no one in California can tell you which teacher is in which category. Something is wrong with that picture.

> **FAST FACT**
>
> In Chicago, Illinois, teachers whose students improve their test scores can earn as much as eight thousand dollars in bonuses, according to *USA Today*. Middle-school math teachers in Nashville, Tennessee, can earn as much as fifteen thousand dollars in bonuses.

I know that many forward-thinking educators share this view and I am confident that, with your help and your thoughtful work, we can overcome the legitimate concerns of teachers that they are being judged merely on test scores. . . .

What Makes Great Teachers?

Which schools of education are producing the teachers that produce the students that improve the most year after year? We need to know that answer.

We can one day do a better job of understanding what makes great teachers tick, why they succeed, why they stay in the classroom and how others can be like them. Hopefully, we can track good programs to higher test scores to higher graduation rates. Hopefully, one day we can look a child in the eye at the age of eight or nine or 10 and say, "You are on track to be accepted and to succeed in a competitive university and, if you keep working hard, you will absolutely get there."

Teacher Assessments of Their Own Instructional Performance

Lacking clear performance standards by which to measure their performance, most teachers in a recent study rated themselves an 8, 9, or 10 on a scale of 10. Almost no teachers rated themselves in the bottom half.

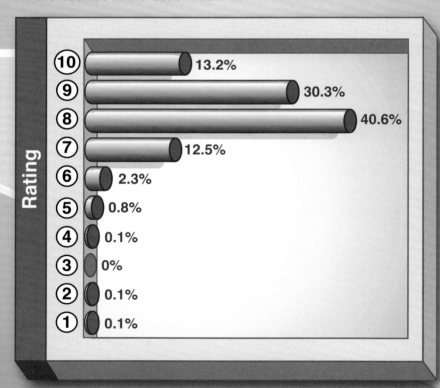

Rating

- (10) 13.2%
- (9) 30.3%
- (8) 40.6%
- (7) 12.5%
- (6) 2.3%
- (5) 0.8%
- (4) 0.1%
- (3) 0%
- (2) 0.1%
- (1) 0.1%

Taken from: The New Teacher Project, *The Widget Effect: Our National Failure to Acknowledge and Act on Differences in Teacher Effectiveness*, 2009.

Today, many states are well along the path to having good data systems. Today, nearly every district has an information system that stores data about students, and more teachers have access to these systems than ever before.

In Garden Grove, California, teachers administer quarterly assessments aligned with California state standards. Results are available the next day.

In Long Beach, teachers see benchmarked assessments, attendance and behavior. They meet regularly together to review data, monitor student progress, and plan strategies for at-risk students. In addition, the high school students monitor their own progress. How is that for motivation? We need more and more districts using this kind of technology to help them improve.

EVALUATING THE AUTHOR'S ARGUMENTS:

The viewpoint you have just read was a speech delivered by the secretary of the U.S. Department of Education to a group of researchers in the government agency the Institute of Education Sciences—that is, a speech delivered by the head of an organization to a group of people who work for him. What language in the viewpoint reflects Arne Duncan's expectation that his audience agrees with him, at least in large part? How does the fact that his primary audience is a group of his employees affect your reading of the viewpoint?

Present Tests Are Not a Good Measurement of a Teacher's Effectiveness

W. James Popham

"In most states, teachers really have no clear idea about what's going to be measured on their state's upcoming accountability tests."

In the following viewpoint, educator W. James Popham argues that test scores are not a fair way to determine which teachers are doing their jobs well. Most state-based standardized tests cover weakly defined content standards, he contends, and teachers and students generally do not know what the tests will, in fact, cover. In addition, he concludes, the tests demonstrate only what students know at one moment in time, not whether they have been taught well. Popham is past president of the American Educational Research Association and the author of *Testing! Testing! What Every Parent Should Know About School Tests* (2000).

W. James Popham, "Test Scores and Teacher Competency," OregonLive.com, February 4, 2010. Reproduced by permission.

AS YOU READ, CONSIDER THE FOLLOWING QUESTIONS:
1. How does the federal Race to the Top program affect how teachers might be evaluated, as reported by Popham?
2. According to the author, what is wrong with the curriculum goals in most states?
3. What is meant by the phrase "instructionally sensitive," as it is used by Popham?

Teachers should be evaluated according to how well their students learn. This is almost as obvious as saying the winner of a football game should be the team that scores the most points. Indeed, the inherent reasonableness of judging teachers by their students' test scores has spurred many policymakers to demand that students' test performances be the dominant factor by which we evaluate a teacher's competence.

In recent weeks, the push toward test-based teacher evaluation has been ratcheted up remarkably because of the federal Race to the Top program [announced in July 2009] in which states have a better chance of receiving dollars if the state's educational leaders agree to make students' test scores a serious factor in how they evaluate their state's teachers. This is surely not the first time the lure of federal largesse has inclined state officials to adopt a stance that, otherwise, might have been rebuffed.

Clear Testing Targets

But judging teachers on the basis of their students' test scores makes sense only if a pair of make-or-break conditions have been satisfied; namely, (1) the presence of clear, teacher-understood testing targets and (2) the use of instructionally sensitive tests. Let's look at both of those necessary requirements, and see why they're so significant.

First, teachers must understand what is going to be tested. It is fundamentally unfair to ask teachers to raise their students' test scores without having a reasonably clear idea of what is eligible to be tested. This would be like asking Olympic gymnasts to perform, but not telling them which factors will be used by the judges who evaluate their performances.

Second, the tests being used must be instructionally sensitive, that is, demonstrably able to distinguish between well-taught students and poorly taught students. Inaccurate estimates of teachers' instructional success will surely be produced if a test can't tell the difference between students who were taught effectively and those students who were taught ineffectively.

If either of these two requirements has not been satisfied, then the use of students' test scores to evaluate teachers is unwarranted. Regrettably, at the moment, in almost all of our 50 states, neither of these requisite conditions has been satisfied. Let's see why.

Assessing States' Math Standard

In 2005 the Thomas B. Fordham Institute reviewed the math curriculum standards in the individual states, evaluating them for clarity, content, and mathematical reasoning. Only three states—California, Indiana, and Massachusetts—earned an "A."

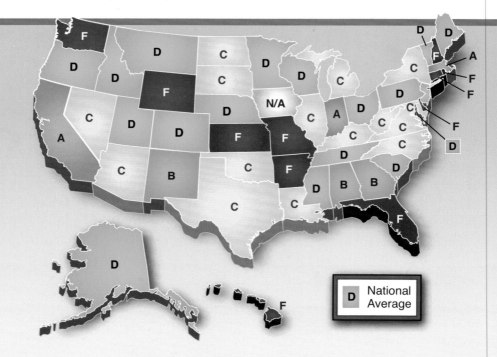

Taken from: Chester E. Finn Jr., Liam Julian, and Michael J. Petrilli, *2006: The State of State Standards* Washington, DC: Thomas B. Fordham Institute, 2006, p. 18.

State Tests Are Inadequate

Currently, most proponents of test-based teacher evaluation want to rely on a state's annual accountability assessments as the tests to be used in this process. The problem with such tests, however, is that they are typically constructed in order to assess students' mastery of a state's officially approved curricular goals.

What's wrong with this seemingly sensible strategy? In a nutshell, most states have regrettably identified far too many curricular aims—too many to be taught in the available teaching time or to be tested in the available testing time. As a consequence, statewide accountability tests have no alternative but to sample the curricular goals to be measured on a given year's tests. Some curricular goals will be assessed annually; some won't.

This situation forces teachers to guess regarding which curricular goals will be tested each year. And, of course, a good deal of inaccurate guessing unavoidably takes place. As a result, many teachers end up emphasizing what isn't tested, and failing to emphasize what actually is tested. In most states, teachers really have no clear idea about what's going to be measured on their state's upcoming accountability tests.

> **FAST FACT**
>
> In "norm-referenced" tests, students are compared with each other; a score of 75 percent, for example, means that the student scored as well as or better than 75 percent of the students taking the test. This means that for any norm-referenced test, half of the students are rated below average.

If teachers truly understand the nature of the skills and bodies of knowledge being assessed, then they can teach toward such skills and knowledge rather than toward a test's items. Teaching to a test's items is deplorable; teaching to the skills and knowledge measured by a test's items is admirable.

The Tests Do Not Measure Teaching

Next, let's look at the instructional sensitivity of the tests that most advocates of test-based teacher evaluation would have us use. An instructionally sensitive test will identify which students have been well

Washington governor Chris Cregoire, right, at a Washington high school, promotes an education bill she designed to help her state get a portion of the Race to the Top program's $4.35 billion in funds to help states.

taught and which students haven't. But, at the moment, there is no evidence whatsoever that the tests being touted for test-based teacher evaluation are up to that task.

State accountability tests, the annually administered standardized tests used as part of a state's accountability tests, are accompanied by no evidence—none at all—that they can tell the difference between students who have been taught well and those who haven't. That's right, there's no documentation that these annual accountability tests are instructionally sensitive. On the contrary, available evidence suggests that today's state accountability tests are instructionally insensitive.

These tests have been constructed using traditional procedures designed to produce comparative score-interpretations, for example, to allow us to say, "Kelly scored at the 78th percentile, that is, outperformed essentially 78 percent of other test-takers." For such tests to provide these sorts of comparative interpretations, however, it is necessary for the tests to produce a considerable amount of spread in students' total test scores.

But to attain such score-spread, many of the items on state account-ability tests end up being linked to students' inherited academic ap-titudes, such as a child's innate quantitative potential, or to the socioeconomic status of a student's family. Because inherited aptitudes and family status are nicely distributed variables, test items influenced by these factors tend to create the needed spread in students' test scores. Yet, inherited academic aptitudes and family status reflect what students bring to school, not what they are taught once they get there. Many of today's accountability tests are laden with items tending to make them instructionally insensitive.

Can these two problems be addressed so we can carry out defensi-ble test-based teacher evaluation? Absolutely! Serious efforts can be made to communicate upcoming testing targets to teachers. Solid ev-idence can be collected to indicate whether a test is, in fact, instruc-tionally sensitive.

Test-based teacher evaluation can be made sensible—but only if we first let teachers know what's going to be tested, and then make sure the tests we use are suitable for this purpose. Otherwise, with or without federal dollars, test-based teacher evaluation will surely be specious.

EVALUATING THE AUTHORS' ARGUMENTS:

In the opening of the viewpoint you have just read, W. James Popham compares teaching and learning to a foot-ball game. Two other authors in this chapter—Walt Gard-ner and Arne Duncan—use sports analogies to explain their ideas about teacher evaluation. How useful is this set of metaphors (even the commonly used image of "setting the bar low" refers to athletics) when describing educa-tion? How is formal education like and unlike an athletic competition?

Viewpoint 5

A National Test Would Support Rigorous Proficiency Standards

Michael K. Smith

"Logically . . . the development of national standards would lead to the development of national tests to measure these common standards."

In the viewpoint that follows, Michael K. Smith proposes a national computer-based test in mathematics, available to anyone from kindergarten to graduate student level. Such a test, he argues, could replace the many standardized mathematics tests now offered to students and the general public for educational and employment purposes and would offer a more consistent way for test takers to measure their skills against common standards and against other test takers. Tests could also be created for other subjects, including reading and science, he maintains. Smith is president of Testprep Experts in Knoxville, Tennessee, and teaches in the Department of Educational Psychology at the University of Tennessee–Knoxville.

Michael K. Smith, "Why Not a National Test for Everyone?" *Phi Delta Kappan*, February 2010, pp. 54–59. Reproduced by permission.

AS YOU READ, CONSIDER THE FOLLOWING QUESTIONS:
1. For whom would the new mathematics test be designed, as proposed by the author?
2. Which groups are already using computer-adaptive tests, according to Smith?
3. How might students and teachers use the proposed public aspect of the new test, according to the author?

Another new movement is gaining momentum to craft "national" standards in mathematics, reading, and writing. Orchestrated by the Council of Chief State School Officers (CCSSO) and the National Governors Association (NGA), these Common Core of Standards could possibly be implemented by all 50 states and serve as the basis of changes to curriculum and assessment. As might be expected, this effort is meeting with both praise and criticism. And, logically, of course, the development of national standards would lead to the development of national tests to measure these common standards.

Because the concept of a national test will very likely emerge from these efforts, I want to propose a more radical, and perhaps broader, vision of what this national test might resemble. I suggest that this national test be designed for "everyone": students, teachers, parents, and citizens of our democracy. This national test could be computer-adaptive, based on standards that span preschool to the Ph.D., set on a common scale and normed to provide average scores at various levels, and have both public and secure administrations. If we take mathematics as a starting point, everyone could have a personal national mathematics score. Students could compare their scores to their teachers' and parents'; workers could compare their scores to other workers' and supervisors'; and, conceivably, students in other nations could compare themselves to students in the United States.

Let me suggest an analogy. The United States Chess Federation has a national rating system that ranks all players, novices to grandmasters. Chess competitions have specific rules for how these ratings are determined. Every player is ranked on a common scale with set levels and criteria for definitions of "expert" and "master." Most computer chess programs have simulated scenarios that allow a player to determine his or her "rating" based on play versus the computer or solution of posed problems.

A Common Barometer

Could we not envision the same system for mathematics? Anyone could sign onto the Internet and be presented with "problems" in mathematics, with the difficulty of the problems adapting to the person's level of ability. After about 30 minutes of problem solving, anyone could see his or her "rating" and, perhaps, be given feedback on its interpretation and steps needed to increase the score. With a large enough item pool, the test could be taken at any time. . . .

One of the educational testing reforms that has been proposed is a national standardized test on the computer via the Internet.

Imagine the scope of a national test that could be used to measure a student's knowledge from kindergarten through high school. The test could also be used to assess college readiness, serve as a college admissions [tool] to measure a person's ability as he or she proceeds through college, graduate work, and into a professional career. Furthermore, the test could be used for employment decisions in such areas as teacher certification and pre-employment screening. The nation would have a common "barometer" of mathematical ability. At one fell swoop, this test could replace all existing state K–12 assessments used under No Child Left Behind [NCLB]; all college barometers, and . . . college admissions tests such as the SAT and ACT; all graduate and professional admissions tests like the GRE, GMAT, and PRAXIS; and entry-level employment measures that test mathematical ability.

Before I'm diagnosed with delusions of grandeur, let me outline the elements of such a system, how it could be constructed and put to use in a relatively brief period of time, and why it would be a practical solution to many educational dilemmas. . . .

The Construction of a National Test

How would this test be constructed and administered? A computer-adaptive format offered through the Internet would have the widest possible access. Computer-adaptive technology has been pioneered and used with the products from many organizations: Educational Testing Service's GRE and GMAT; Northwest Educational Association's MAP [Measures of Academic Progress] product for K–12; and the screening and certification exams of many professional and military groups. . . .

A student, teacher, or citizen could sign onto the Internet to take this national test. First, responses to a few screening items would estimate the person's starting point in the educational continuum or the person's highest level of education could serve as the beginning. As items are administered and scored, the computer "adapts" to a person's ability level. If a person answers items correctly, he or she is given questions of greater difficulty until his or her ability level is reached. If a person answers items incorrectly, he or she is presented with questions of lesser difficulty. The selection of items alternates between easy and hard until a final estimate of a person's ability is reached. The Graduate Record Examination's Quantitative computer-adaptive test estimates a person's ability for graduate school mathematical reasoning with 28 questions in a 45-minute time frame. The national test in mathematics could easily be modeled on this method. Thus, anyone could obtain his or her "rating" in less than an hour.

How could we trust this "rating?" And how would anyone "practice" for this important national test? This national test could have both a "public" and "secure" component. The public element would consist of an item bank of several thousand high-quality items that have been written to standards and ranked on difficulty. In this public element, anyone at anytime could obtain an estimate of his or her mathematical ability. The secure portion would contain a different item bank of thousands of quality items. This secure portion could be used for accountability purposes and be administered only in "controlled" settings.

The public aspect would be open to anyone at anytime. Teachers and students could use it for practice and skill building throughout the school year. Colleges and businesses could use the material to strengthen student and employee skills. Citizens and parents could improve their own grasp of mathematics at home. Access to the secure site could be granted to any organization that needs a score for accountability, placement, or promotion. This type of access is not hard to imagine. Right now, many computer-adaptive tests are given in controlled settings to ensure the integrity of the measurement process. The national test could follow this model. . . .

How would these "scores" on the national test be interpreted? How high a score would be appropriate for 7th graders? What level might be needed for college admission? How much mathematics is needed for entry-level jobs?

As with any standardized test, a process of collecting averages or norms would be put in place. . . .

Extensions to Other Domains

If we can imagine a national test in mathematics along the lines presented here, is it not feasible to envision tests in other domains? Skills in reading comprehension and language arts, so much a part of NCLB, could be assessed with their own national tests. Furthermore, basic knowledge in science, history, geography, economics, and literature could be ascertained in this format. Skill in foreign language reading, grammar, and even listening comprehension could be presented and tested through these same means.

EVALUATING THE AUTHOR'S ARGUMENTS:

Michael K. Smith is an enthusiastic advocate for the kind of computer-based test he is proposing, and he clearly explains step by step how it would work and the advantages it would offer. Can you envision any downside to the plan he proposes? What challenges might individual citizens, families, or school districts have to overcome to adopt Smith's plan?

Standardized Tests Do Not Accurately Measure Proficiency

Chester E. Finn Jr. and Michael J. Petrilli

"Mr. and Mrs. Smith know that little Susie is 'proficient.' What they don't know is that 'proficient' doesn't mean much."

In the following viewpoint, researchers Chester E. Finn Jr. and Michael J. Petrilli argue that standardized tests reveal much less about a student's knowledge and skills than most people think they do. Because the nebulous word *proficiency* carries a different meaning in different states, they contend, a student's score on a state-based standardized test does not yield objective information about that student's achievements. The educational establishment, they conclude, has become too reliant on gathering and processing data, without asking the important questions about what such data mean. Finn is the president of the Thomas B. Fordham Institute, a think tank dedicated to advancing educational excellence in America's K–12 schools. Petrilli is the institute's vice president for national programs and policy.

AS YOU READ, CONSIDER THE FOLLOWING QUESTIONS:
1. As defined by Finn and Petrilli, what is a "proficiency passing score"?
2. How do most people define educational success, according to the authors?
3. How do the passing levels for eighth-grade reading in South Carolina compare with those in Wisconsin, according to Finn and Petrilli?

No Child Left Behind [NCLB] made many promises, one of the most important of them being a pledge to Mr. and Mrs. Smith that they would get an annual snapshot of how their little Susie is doing in school. Mr. and Mrs. Taxpayer would get an honest appraisal of how their local schools and school system are faring. Ms. Brown, Susie's teacher, would get helpful feedback from her pupils' annual testing data. And the children themselves would benefit, too. As President [George W.] Bush explained last year [2006] during a school visit, "One of the things that I think is most important about the No Child Left Behind Act is that when you measure, particularly in the early grades, it enables you to address an individual's problem today, rather than try to wait until tomorrow. My attitude is, is that measuring early enables a school to correct problems early . . . measuring is the gateway to success."

So far so good; these are the ideas that underpin twenty years of sensible education reform. But let's return to little Susie Smith and whether the information coming to her parents and teachers is truly reliable and trustworthy: This fourth-grader lives in suburban Detroit, and her parents get word that she has passed Michigan's state test. She's "proficient" in reading and math. Mr. and Mrs. Smith understandably take this as good news; their daughter must be "on grade level" and on track to do well in later grades of school, maybe even go to college.

Would that it were so. Unfortunately, there's a lot that Mr. and Mrs. Smith don't know. They don't know that Michigan set its "proficiency passing score"—the score a student must attain in order to pass the test—among the lowest in the land. So Susie may be "proficient" in math in the eyes of Michigan education bureaucrats but she still could have scored worse than five-sixths of the other fourth-graders in the country. Susie's parents and teachers also don't know that Michigan has set the bar particularly low for younger students, such that Susie is likely to fail the state test by the time she gets to sixth grade—and certainly when she reaches eighth grade—even if she makes regular progress every year. And they also don't know that "proficiency" on Michigan's state tests has little meaning outside the Wolverine State's

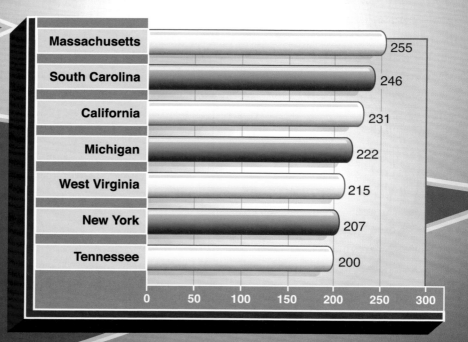

State Math Standards Are Not Uniform

Individual state standards for fourth-grade mathematics vary widely. This chart shows the estimated scores students would have earned on the National Assessment of Educational Progress (NAEP) exam if they achieved their own states' "proficiency passing scores," or lowest requirements for proficiency, in 2005.

State	Estimated NAEP score
Massachusetts	255
South Carolina	246
California	231
Michigan	222
West Virginia	215
New York	207
Tennessee	200

Estimated NAEP score equivalent to the state standard.

Taken from: U.S. Department of Education, *Mapping 2005 State Proficiency Standards onto the NAEP Scales*, Institute of Education Sciences, 2007.

borders; if Susie lived in California or Massachusetts or South Carolina, she would have missed the "proficiency" cut-off by a mile.

Mr. and Mrs. Smith know that little Susie is "proficient." What they don't know is that "proficient" doesn't mean much. This is the proficiency illusion. . . .

Weak and Nebulous Standards

We've known for years that there's a problem with many states' academic standards—the aspirational statements, widely available on state websites, of what students at various grade levels should know and be able to do in particular subjects. Fordham [the Thomas B. Fordham Institute] has been appraising state standards since 1997. A few states do a super job, yet our most recent comprehensive review (2006) found that "two-thirds of schoolchildren in America attend class in states with mediocre (or worse) expectations for what their students should learn."

Instead of setting forth a coherent sequence of skills and content that comprise the essential learnings of a given subject—and doing so in concrete, cumulative terms that send clear signals to educators, parents, and policymakers—many states settle for nebulous, content-lite standards of scant value to those who are supposed to benefit from them.

That's a serious problem, striking at the very heart of results-based educational accountability. If the desired outcomes of schooling aren't well stated, what is the likelihood that they will be produced?

Yet that problem turns out to be just the opening chapter of an alarming tale. For we also understood that, when it comes to the real traction of standards-based education reform, a state's posted academic standards aren't the most important element. What really drives behavior, determines results, and shapes how performance is reported and understood, is the passing level—also known as the "cut score"—on the states actual tests. At day's end, most people define educational success by how many kids pass the state test and how many fail. No matter what the aspirational statements set forth as goals, the rubber meets the road when the testing program determines that Susie (or Michelle or Caleb or Tyrone or Rosa) is or is not "proficient" as determined by their scores on state assessments.

The advent of high-stakes testing in general, and No Child Left Behind in particular, have underscored this. When NCLB asks whether a school or district is making "adequate yearly progress" in a given year, what it's really asking is whether an acceptable number of children scored at (or above) the "proficient" level as specified on the state's tests—and how many failed to do so. . . .

Awash in Data

What does this mean for educational policy and practice? What does it mean for standards-based reform in general and NCLB in particular? It means big trouble—and those who care about strengthening U.S. K–12 education should be furious. There's all this testing—too much, surely—yet the testing enterprise is unbelievably slipshod. It's not just that results vary, but that they vary almost randomly, erratically, from place to place and grade to grade and year to year in ways that have little or nothing to do with true differences in pupil achievement. America is awash in achievement "data," yet the truth about our educational performance is far from transparent and trustworthy. It may be smoke and mirrors. Gains (and slippages) may be illusory. Comparisons may be misleading. Apparent problems may be nonexistent or, at least, misstated. The testing infrastructure on which so many school reform efforts rest, and in which so much confidence has been vested, is unreliable—at best. We believe in results-based, test-measured, standards-aligned accountability systems. They're the core of NCLB, not to mention earlier (and concurrent) systems devised by individual states. But it turns out that there's far more to trust here than we, and you, and lawmakers have assumed. Indeed, the policy implications are sobering. First, we see that Congress erred big-time when NCLB assigned each state to set its own standards and devise and score its own tests; no matter what one thinks of America's history of state primacy in K–12 education, this study underscores the folly of a big modern nation, worried about its global competitiveness, nodding with approval as Wisconsin sets its eighth-grade reading passing level at the 14th percentile while South Carolina sets its at the 71st percentile. A youngster moving from middle school in Boulder [Colorado] to high school in Charleston [South Carolina] would be grievously unprepared for what lies ahead. So would a child moving from third grade in Detroit [Michigan] to fourth grade in Albuquerque [New Mexico]. . . .

Standards-based reform hinges on the assumption that one can trust the standards, that they are stable anchors to which the educational accountability vessel is moored. If the anchor doesn't hold firm, the vessel moves—and if the anchor really slips, the vessel can crash against the rocks or be lost at sea.

That, we now see clearly, is the dire plight of standards-based reform in the United States today.

EVALUATING THE AUTHORS' ARGUMENTS:

In the viewpoint you have just read, the authors use a combination of technical jargon and simple language: They include references to "standards-based education reform" and "aspirational statements," as well as the anecdote about little Susie. How does this approach help them appeal to different readers? How does the story of the Smith family affect the way you read the viewpoint?

Chapter 3

Are Standardized Tests Valuable for College Admissions?

Students take a standardized test at a university.

Viewpoint 1

Achievement Tests Are Good Tools for College Admissions

Richard C. Atkinson and Saul Geiser

"Curriculum-based achievement tests are the fairest and most effective assessments for college admissions."

In the following viewpoint, Richard C. Atkinson and Saul Geiser argue that the most useful standardized tests for college admissions are tests that are directly tied to what students are expected to learn in high school. Trying to predict which students will do well in college has failed, they claim, but standardized tests can serve other purposes. The authors conclude that well-crafted achievement tests can help high school students understand that they must work hard in school, and they can help colleges and universities expand the pool of students they judge to be good candidates for admission. Atkinson is a former president of the University of California; Geiser is a research associate with the Center for Studies in Higher Education.

Richard C. Atkinson and Saul Geiser, "Reflections on a Century of College Admissions Tests," Center for Studies in Higher Education, April 2009. Reproduced by permission.

AS YOU READ, CONSIDER THE FOLLOWING QUESTIONS:

1. How many high school seniors take the SAT or ACT each year, as reported by Atkinson and Geiser?
2. According to the authors, what is the best indicator of student readiness for college?
3. When Atkinson and Geiser call for tests that are "criterion-referenced," what are they saying admissions tests should reveal about students?

Standardized testing for college admissions has seen extraordinary growth over the past century and appears on the cusp of still more far-reaching changes. Fewer than 1,000 examinees sat for the first "College Boards" in 1901. Today nearly three million high-school seniors take the SAT or ACT each year. And this does not count many more who take preliminary versions of college-entrance tests earlier in school or sit for the exams multiple times, nor does it include those who take the SAT Subject Tests and Advanced Placement exams. Admissions testing continues to be a growth industry, and further innovations such as computer-based assessments with instant scoring, adaptive testing, and "non-cognitive" assessment are poised to make their appearance.

FAST FACT

Harvard University requires applicants to submit SAT or ACT scores but also requires scores on three College Board Subject Tests, which measure academic achievement in particular subject areas.

Despite this growth and apparent success, however, the feeling persists that all is not well in the world of admissions testing. College-entrance tests and related test-preparation activities have contributed mightily to what one of us [Atkinson] has called the "educational arms race"—the ferocious competition for admission at highly selective institutions. Many deserving low-income and minority students are squeezed out in this competition, and questions about fairness and equity are raised with increasing urgency. The role of the testing agencies themselves has also come into question, and some ask whether the testing industry holds too much sway over the colleges and universities it purports to serve. Underlying all of these questions is a deeper concern that the current regime of admissions testing may impede rather than advance our educational purpose. . . .

Our thesis, in brief, is this: The original College Boards started out as achievement tests, designed to assess students' mastery of college-preparatory subjects. A century of admissions testing has taught us that this initial premise may have been sounder than anyone realized at the time. After a prolonged detour with alternative approaches to

Students in a prep class prepare for college entrance exams. A century of admission testing has shown that assessing a student's mastery of college preparatory subjects works best in determining college admissions.

admissions testing, today we have come full circle to a renewed appreciation for the value of achievement tests. But the journey has been useful, since we now have a much better understanding of *why* assessment of achievement and curriculum mastery remains vital as a paradigm for admissions testing. Curriculum-based achievement tests are the fairest and most effective assessments for college admissions and have important incentive or "signaling" effects for our K–12 schools as well: They help reinforce a rigorous academic curriculum and create better alignment of teaching, learning, and assessment all along the pathway from high school to college.

Putting Tests in Perspective

A first order of business is to put admissions tests in proper perspective: High-school grades are the best indicator of student readiness for college, and standardized tests are useful primarily as a supplement to the high-school record.

High-school grades are sometimes viewed as a less reliable indicator than standardized tests because grading standards differ across schools. The reality is different. Though it is true that grading standards vary by school, grades still outperform standardized tests in predicting college outcomes: Irrespective of the quality or type of school attended, cumulative grade-point average in academic subjects in high school has proven consistently the best overall predictor of student performance in college. This finding has been confirmed in hundreds of "predictive-validity" studies conducted over the years, including studies conducted by the testing agencies themselves. . . .

In contrast to prediction, the idea of achievement offers a richer paradigm for admissions testing and calls attention to a broader array of characteristics that we should demand of our tests:

- Admissions tests should be *criterion-referenced* rather than norm-referenced: Our primary consideration should not be how an applicant compares with others but whether he or she demonstrates sufficient mastery of college-preparatory subjects to benefit from and succeed in college.
- Admissions tests should have *diagnostic utility*: Rather than a number or a percentile rank, tests should provide students with curriculum-related information about areas of strength as well as areas where they need to devote more study.

- Admissions tests should exhibit not only predictive validity but *face validity*: The relationship between the knowledge and skills being tested and those needed for college should be transparent.
- Admissions tests should be *aligned with high-school curricula*: Assessments should be linked as closely as possible to materials that students encounter in the classroom and should reinforce teaching and learning of rigorous college-preparatory curriculum in our schools.
- Admissions tests should *minimize the need for test preparation*: Though test-prep services will probably never disappear entirely, admissions tests should be designed to reward mastery of curriculum content over test-taking skills, so that the best test-prep is regular classroom instruction.
- Finally and most important, admissions tests should send a *signal to students*: Our tests should send the message that working hard and mastering academic subjects in high school is the most direct route to college. . . .

When we judge students against this standard, two truths become evident. First is that the pool of qualified candidates who could benefit from and succeed in college is far larger than can be accommodated at selective institutions. Second is that admissions criteria other than test scores—special talents and skills, leadership and community service, opportunity to learn, economic disadvantage, and social and cultural diversity—are far more important in selecting whom to admit from among this larger pool. Admissions officers often describe their work as "crafting a class," a phrase that nicely captures this meaning.

Achievement testing reflects a philosophy of admissions that is at once more modest and at the same time more expansive than predicting success in college. It is more modest in that it asks less of admissions tests and is more realistic about what they can do: Our ability to predict success in college is relatively limited, and the most we should ask of admissions tests is to certify students' mastery of foundational knowledge and skills. But it also suggests a more expansive vision: Beyond some reasonable standard of college readiness, other admissions criteria must take precedence over test scores if we are to craft an entering class that reflects our broader institutional values. And beyond the relatively narrow world of selective college admissions, testing for achievement and curriculum mastery can have a broader and more beneficial "signaling effect" throughout all of education.

Standardized Tests Are Overemphasized in College Admissions

Elizabeth Landau

"Applicants may take too much time on prepping for this test and their time can be better spent dedicating themselves to other activities."

In the following viewpoint, Elizabeth Landau explains why many colleges and universities have decided to deemphasize test scores when deciding which students to admit. Research has shown, she writes, that students with lower incomes and minority students do less well on the tests than their peers, although they may be just as ready to benefit from a college education. It may even improve a school's image, argues a consultant quoted in the viewpoint, to demonstrate a concern for diversity rather than for test scores. Landau is a writer and producer for CNN News.

Elizabeth Landau, "More Colleges Move Toward Optional SATs," CNN.com, May 20, 2008. Reproduced by permission.

AS YOU READ, CONSIDER THE FOLLOWING QUESTIONS:
1. According to the author, what is the most widely used college admissions exam in the United States?
2. Who argues that the SAT "is a critical tool for success," as quoted by Landau?
3. How did some schools react to the revised SAT test that came out in 2005, as reported by the author?

Jen Wang of Short Hills, New Jersey, took her first SAT when she was in sixth grade, long before she would start filling out college applications.

"My family thought it was very important for me to do well on this test, and I basically obtained nearly every SAT study guide out there by the time I was a junior in high school," she said. "For Christmas one year, I received an electronic device that allowed me to practice the SAT's 'on-the-go.'"

After all that preparation, she ended up attending a school that has made the SAT Reasoning Test, generally known as the SAT, the most widely used college admissions exam in the United States, optional.

The SAT and Income

Her school, Connecticut College, is one of a growing number of colleges and universities that are making the SAT optional in the admissions process. In May, two highly selective schools—Smith College in Massachusetts and Wake Forest University in North Carolina—decided to drop the SAT and ACT, which some students take as an alternative to the SAT, as requirements for admission.

Wake Forest made the move as part of its efforts to increase socioeconomic, racial and ethnic diversity in the student body, said Martha Allman, director of admissions. Research has shown that SAT performance is linked with family income, and that the test by itself does not accurately predict success in college, she said.

Making the test optional "removes the barrier for those students who had everything else," like scholastic achievement and extracurricular activities, but who "maybe didn't do as well on a specific test," she said.

Smith College also cited the correlation between test scores and income as a motivation for making the exam optional, as well as a desire to take a more well-rounded view of applications. The changes at Smith and Wake Forest [took] effect for applicants seeking to enroll in the fall of 2009.

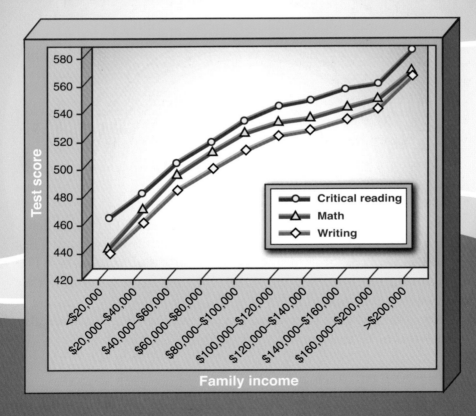

SAT Scores and Family Income

Nearly 1 million college-bound seniors who took the SAT test in 2009 reported their family income. The data show that higher family income is associated with higher scores, on average.

Taken from: College Board, 2009.

A Barrier to Equal Opportunity

Several colleges and universities went test-optional in the 1990s amid concern that the test was a barrier to equal opportunity for minorities, women and low-income students, said Robert Schaeffer, public education director for FairTest. Some schools also dropped the test as a requirement with the explosion of test coaching, which gave upper-income kids an advantage.

About 30 percent, or nearly 760 colleges and universities out of the approximately 2,500 accredited four-year institutions across America, have made at least some standardized tests optional for some applicants, according to the non-profit advocacy group FairTest.

Some of those schools, such as George Mason University in Virginia, still require the tests for prospective students who do not meet a particular GPA requirement in high school.

But Alana Klein, spokesperson for the College Board, which owns the SAT, said this is not a trend. While the news media have focused on recent moves to make the test optional, schools have been doing this for decades, and SAT test volumes are up 2 percent from last year [2007], she said.

The poor performance of some low-income and minority students has to do with their lack of access to quality education, which is a national problem, but does not relate to the test itself, Klein said. The SAT is a fair test for all students, she said, and any test question that shows bias is removed.

"Not only is the SAT a critical tool for success in college, but also in the workforce and in life," she said.

> ## FAST FACT
>
> The National Center for Fair and Open Testing reports that more than 830 four-year colleges and universities do not require ACT or SAT scores for admitting most students.

A Way to Compare Students

At Bowdoin College, which hasn't required the SAT since 1969, the biggest benefit of the test-optional policy is the school's "unusually supportive community" where students don't compare scores, said William Shain, dean of admissions and financial aid.

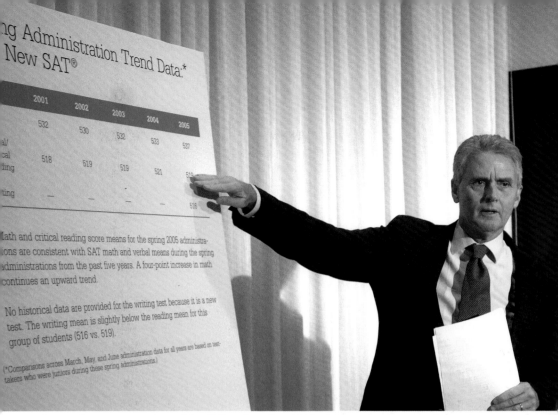

Gaston Caperton, president of the College Board in 2005, discusses in a news conference how the new SAT test will work. Many schools decided not to use the new test in admissions criteria because they thought it did not address their concerns.

But at this small liberal arts college in Maine, which admitted about 18 percent of applicants [in 2008], more than 80 percent of applicants submit scores anyway, he said.

One of the downsides of keeping standardized tests optional is that it's harder to evaluate a large pool of candidates who all have high GPAs, he said.

Richard Atkinson, former president of the University of California, recommended in 2001 that the school system no longer require the SAT Reasoning Test for admission. He cited the concerns of African-Americans and Hispanics that these groups tend to perform worse on the exam than students of other ethnicities.

"The real basis of their concern, however, is that they have no way of knowing what the SAT measures and, therefore, have no basis for assessing its fairness or helping their children acquire the skills to do better," Atkinson said in 2001. The University of California system still requires the test today.

Several other schools dropped the test requirement for admissions after the revised SAT came out in 2005, after seeing that the new version did not address concerns about access and poor predictive value, FairTest's Schaeffer said.

Since spring 2005, 34 colleges and universities have made standardized testing optional for all applicants, according to FairTest. Four others made the requirement optional for students with a lower GPA, FairTest's data showed.

About 25 percent of liberal arts colleges have made a move in the test-optional direction, said Jack Maguire, chairman and founder of Maguire Associates. His consulting firm has advised certain colleges to become test-optional.

"I do think it improves a school's image," he said. "It shows what's important to schools, if they're really interested in increasing diversity."

Wang, who just finished her freshman year at Connecticut College, said she is torn on the SAT debate—the test sharpened her vocabulary and test-taking skills, but preparation took up a lot of time that could have been spent doing other things.

"Applicants may take too much time on prepping for this test and their time can be better spent dedicating themselves to other activities that could show colleges what the applicants really find meaningful in their lives," she said.

> ## EVALUATING THE AUTHOR'S ARGUMENTS:
>
> The viewpoint you have just read is unusual in that it quotes a student giving her opinion about the issue at hand; in this volume, the only other viewpoint to include the voices of students is the viewpoint by Monty Neill in Chapter 1. What is the value—and what are the limitations—of quoting students when arguing about matters of educational policy and practice? Why do most authors focus on the views of researchers, teachers, and administrators instead?

The SAT Is a Good Predictor of College Success

Peter Salins

> *"Those campuses whose SAT scores improved substantially . . . saw gains in the most valid measure of academic success: graduation rates."*

In the following viewpoint, former university provost Peter Salins argues that students' scores on standardized tests—particularly on the SAT—are better predictors of college success than high school grades. At the large State University of New York (SUNY) system, where he was responsible for university-wide academic planning and standards, several campuses took deliberate steps to accept students with higher SAT scores, he reports, and these schools saw their undergraduate graduation rates increase substantially. The data clearly show, he concludes, that test scores are more valuable than grades in identifying students who are likely to complete a college degree. Salins is now a professor of political science at SUNY Stony Brook.

Peter Salins, "Does the SAT Predict College Success?" *Minding the Campus*, October 15, 2008. Reproduced by permission.

One of the hottest debates roiling American campuses today is whether the SAT and other standardized tests should continue to play a dominant role as a college admissions criterion. The main point of contention in this debate is whether the SAT or equivalent scores accurately gauge college preparedness, and whether they are valid predictors of college success, most particularly in comparison with high school grades. . . .

Let's dive into the empirical heart of the controversy: whether SAT or similar tests predict collegiate academic success with reasonable accuracy. In making such a determination, we need first to have a way of measuring it. Given enormous variability in the rigor and grading standards of college courses, the best possible metric of academic success is degree completion. From the perspective of both students and society, the reason to go to college is to earn a degree, a goal whose importance is reinforced by national data that indicates the enormous economic premium associated with possessing a baccalaureate. So the empirical question behind the SAT debate can be phrased thus: how strongly are baccalaureate graduation rates correlated with students' admissions test scores, especially when compared to similar correlations based on high school grade point averages.

Fortunately, we can find answers to this question by looking at the experience of the largest university system in the United States—the State University of New York (SUNY) with over 200,000 students enrolled in its sixteen baccalaureate colleges and research universities; a set of distinctive campuses with highly varied student profiles and admissions requirements. As provost of SUNY for many years, I was deeply involved in reviewing campus and admissions criteria, and I

One of the hot debates on standardized testing is whether the SAT and other standardized tests should continue to play a dominant role in college admission criteria.

oversaw the university's institutional research operation, which maintains a comprehensive student unit record system. Given the sheer scale of SUNY, and the diversity among its campuses with respect to admissions criteria and student academic outcomes, we have a controlled experiment of sorts.

During the period that I served as Provost, all campuses were encouraged to clarify their admissions criteria and, once having decided on a specified level of selectivity, to be consistent in implementing it. Many campuses opted to remain in their historic selectivity tier (which can be characterized as "intermediate" relative to national peers), but a significant number chose to raise their admissions standards. The SUNY admissions selectivity template considers both an applicant's high school grade point average (GPA) and his/her SAT or equivalent standardized test scores, but campuses looking to raise their admissions standards focused more on SAT scores than grades. High school GPAs at SUNY have been remarkably consistent both across campuses and over time. Thus, by comparing graduation rates at SUNY campuses that raised the SAT admissions bar with those that didn't—in the context of more or less stable high school grades—we can get a pretty clear idea of whether higher SAT scores lead to higher graduation rates.

The short answer is: they do. Looking at changes in admissions profiles and 6 year graduation rates of the entering classes of 1997 and 2001 at SUNY's 16 baccalaureate institutions, a period during which some campuses became more selective and others did not, this is what we find. Among this group—encompassing a broad band of selectivity from nearly open admissions to highly selective—nine campuses chose to increase their selectivity after 1997. This group included two nationally ranked research universities (Buffalo, Stony Brook) and seven regional colleges (Brockport, Cortland, New Paltz, Old Westbury, Oneonta, Potsdam and Purchase). As noted, the move to raise selectivity standards had a much greater impact on entering students' SAT scores than on their GPAs. For the rising selectivity campuses, SAT score increases between 1997 and 2001 ranged from 4.5 percent (Cortland) to 13.3 percent (Old Westbury), while high school GPAs increased only between 2.4 and 3.7 percent, a gain almost identical to that at campuses that chose not to raise their SAT standards.

The percentage increases in six year graduation rates at the rising selectivity campuses—just over a four year period—were dramatic, ranging between 10 percent (at Stony Brook whose graduation rate went from 53.8 to 59.2) to *95 percent* (at Old Westbury which went from 18.4 to 35.9). Most revealingly, the seven SUNY campuses that stuck with their prior selectivity profiles, meaning their entering students' SAT scores between 1997 and 2001 were stable or rose only modestly, actually saw their graduation rates decline. Even Binghamton, always the most selective of SUNY's research universities, maintained a flat SAT profile and saw its graduation rates decline by 2.8 percent. The most compelling evidence that higher SAT scores predict higher graduation rates can be gleaned by looking at the experiences of campuses with nearly identical student profiles in 1997.

I will highlight the graduation rate experiences of three pairs of comparable SUNY campuses that, between 1997 and 2001, took divergent paths with respect to SAT admissions: two research universities with about 17,000 students (Stony Brook/Albany), two large urban colleges (Brockport/Oswego) with enrollment of about 8,000, and two 5000 student small town liberal arts colleges (Oneonta/Plattsburgh). In each case, in 1997 these pairs had similar admissions profiles with respect to high school GPAs (high 80s for the universities; mid-80s for the colleges). The only distinguishing difference among the campuses in each pair was that by 2001, one school admitted freshmen with significantly higher SAT scores, and the other one didn't. At all of these schools high school GPAs of entering freshman rose modestly between 1997 and 2001: about 2 percent.

In each case, the campus that raised its SAT bar saw a substantial gain in graduation rates—in only four years! . . .

> ## FAST FACT
>
> The Scholastic Aptitude Test was created in 1926. To reflect a new emphasis on achievement rather than aptitude, the name was changed in 1990 to the "Scholastic Assessment Test." Since 1996 the name has been SAT, and the initials do not stand for anything.

SUNY Campuses: SAT Scores and Graduation Rates, 1997–2001

Between 1997 and 2001, on campuses in the State University of New York system, higher increases in average SAT scores for entering freshmen correlated with higher increases in graduation rates.

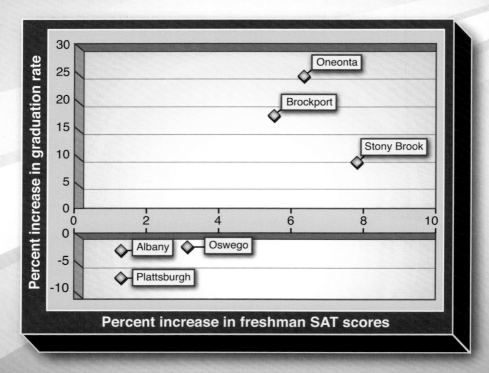

Taken from: Peter Salins, "Does the SAT Predict College Success?" *Minding the Campus*, October 15, 2008.

Other examples: SUNY Old Westbury, always the university system's academically weakest campus, was able to improve its graduation rate by over 95 percent in four years after it instituted higher SAT requirements, increasing its entering students' SAT scores by 13.3 percent between 1997 and 2001. Purchase College, a highly specialized place centered on the fine and performing arts, increased SAT scores by 10.3 percent, and saw graduation rates rise by 22.4 percent.

The common denominator in all of these SUNY examples is that among campuses with highly differentiated missions, across a very wide band of admissions selectivity, all enrolling freshmen whose high school grade point averages improved by the same modest amount (about 2 to 3 percent), only those campuses whose SAT scores improved substantially over this very brief four year interval saw gains in the most valid measure of academic success: graduation rates.

EVALUATING THE AUTHOR'S ARGUMENTS:

The viewpoint you have just read contains a significant amount of data: grade point averages, SAT scores, increase percentages, graduation rates, enrollment figures, and so on. What are the advantages and disadvantages of presenting so much data in support of an argument? How are different audiences likely to respond to this viewpoint's approach?

The SAT Is a Poor Predictor of College Success

National Center for Fair and Open Testing

"The SAT I has little value in predicting future college perform- ance."

In the following viewpoint, the National Center for Fair and Open Testing argues that standardized tests—in particular the SAT Reasoning Test, or SAT I—have little value in terms of predicting how well a prospective student will do in college. Other information available to college admissions officers, including high school grades, class rank, and even students' attitudes, can give colleges a clearer sense of whether students will do well. Because the tests are such poor predictors, and because they particularly un- derestimate the potential of women, non- white students, and older students, colleges should make submission of test scores op- tional, the author concludes. The National Center for Fair and Open Testing, also known as FairTest, is an advocacy organiza- tion that works for quality education and equal opportunity.

"SAT I: A Faulty Instrument for Predicting College Success," FairTest, August 20, 2007. Reproduced by permission.

AS YOU READ, CONSIDER THE FOLLOWING QUESTIONS:

1. What, according to the author, is the SAT I designed to predict?
2. Why is it difficult to reach conclusions about how well the SAT I predicts college success for students of color, according to the author?
3. Why might older or "non-traditional" students perform poorly on the SAT I test, according to the Educational Testing Service, as cited by the author?

Promotional claims for the SAT I [the SAT Reasoning Test] frequently tout the test's important place in the "toolbox" of college admissions officers trying to distinguish between students from vastly different high schools. Yet the true utility of the SAT I is frequently lost in this rhetoric as admissions offices search for a fair and accurate way to compare one student to another. Many colleges and universities around the country, in dropping their test score requirements, have recently confirmed what the research has shown all along—the SAT I has little value in predicting future college performance.

What is the SAT I supposed to measure?

The SAT I is designed to predict first-year college grades—it is not validated to predict grades beyond the freshman year, graduation rates, pursuit of a graduate degree, or for placement or advising purposes. However, according to research done by the tests' manufacturers, class rank and/or high school grades are still both better predictors of college performance than the SAT I. . . .

What do the SAT I validity studies from major colleges and universities show?

Validity research at individual institutions illustrates the weak predictive ability of the SAT. One study at the University of Pennsylvania looked at the power of high school class rank, SAT I, and SAT II [SAT Subject Tests] in predicting cumulative college GPAs. Researchers found that the SAT I was by far the weakest predictor, explaining only 4% of the variation in college grades, while SAT II scores accounted for 6.8% of the differences in academic performance. By far the most useful tool proved to be class rank, which predicted 9.3% of the changes in cumulative GPAs. Combining SAT I scores and class rank inched this figure up to 11.3%, leaving almost 90% of the variation in grades unexplained.

Another study of 10,000 students at 11 selective public and private institutions of higher education found that a 100-point increase in SAT combined scores, holding race, gender, and field of study constant, led to a one-tenth of a grade point gain for college GPA. This offered about the same predictive value as looking at whether an applicant's father had a graduate degree or her mother had completed college. . . .

Bates College, which dropped all pre-admission testing requirements in 1990, first conducted several studies to determine the most powerful variables for predicting success at the college. One study showed that students' self-evaluation of their "energy and initiative"

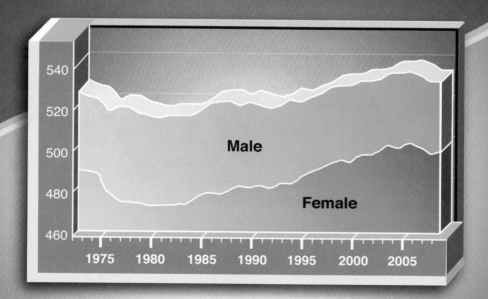

SAT Math Scores: Male vs. Female, 1971–2008

On the mathematics portion of the SAT I test, male students have consistently scored higher than their female peers since the 1970s.

Taken from: College Board.

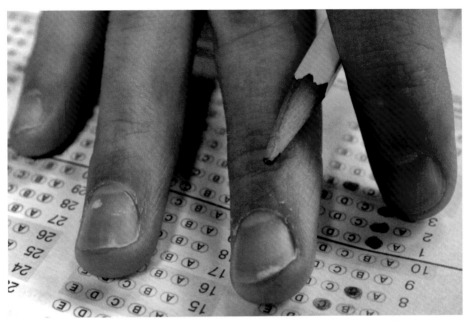

The SAT I test is designed to predict only first-year college grades. It is not valid in predicting grades beyond the freshman year or future graduation rates.

added more to the ability to predict performance at Bates than did either Math or Verbal SAT scores. In comparing five years of enrollees who submitted SAT scores with those who didn't, Bates found that while "non-submitters" averaged 160 points lower on the SAT I, their freshman GPA was only five one-hundredths of a point lower than that of "submitters."

How well does the SAT I predict success beyond the freshman year?

If one looks beyond college grades, information from *The Case Against the SAT* by James Crouse and Dale Trusheim actually points to the SAT I's poor utility in forecasting long-term success. Data they analyzed demonstrated that using the high school record alone to predict who would complete a bachelor's degree resulted in "correct" admissions decisions 73.4% of the time, while using the SAT I and high school GPA forecast "correct" admissions in 72.2% of the cases.

How well does the SAT I predict college achievement for females, students of color, and older students?

The poor predictive ability of the SAT I becomes particularly apparent when considering the college performance of females. Longstanding gaps in scores between males and females of all races show that females on average score 35–40 points lower than males on the SAT I, but receive better high school and college grades. In other words, the test consistently under-predicts the performance of females in college while over-predicting that of males.

Measuring the SAT I's predictive ability for students of color is more complicated since racial classifications are arbitrary. For students whose first language isn't English, test-maker research shows the SAT I frequently under-predicts their future college performance. One study at the University of Miami compared Hispanic and non-Hispanic White students. Though both groups earned equivalent college grades, the Hispanic students received on average combined SAT I scores that were 91 points lower than their non-Hispanic White peers. This gap existed despite the fact that 89% of the Hispanic students reported English as their best language.

FAST FACT

Only 63 percent of entering college freshmen graduate within six years, according to the U.S. Department of Education.

Extensive research compiled by Derek Bok and William Bowen in *The Shape of the River* highlights the SAT I's questionable predictive power for African-American students. The ability of SAT I scores to predict freshman grades, undergraduate class rank, college graduation rates, and attainment of a graduate degree is weaker for African-American students than for Whites. Such discrepancies call into question the usefulness of using the SAT I to assess African-American students' potential.

The SAT I also does a poor job of forecasting the future college performance of older students. ETS [Educational Testing Service, which administers the SAT] acknowledges that the test's predictive power is lower for "non-traditional" students who may be out of practice taking timed, multiple-choice exams. For this reason, many colleges and universities do not require applicants who have been out of high school for five years or more, or those over age 25, to submit test scores. . . .

What's the alternative?

The weak predictive power of the SAT I, its susceptibility to coaching, examples of test score misuse, and the negative impact test score use has on educational equity all lead to the same conclusion—test scores should be optional in college admissions. The nearly 400 colleges and universities that already admit substantial numbers of freshman applicants without regard to test scores have shown that class rank, high school grades, and rigor of classes taken are better tools for predicting college success than any standardized test. The ACT and SAT II are often viewed as alternatives to the SAT I. While they are more closely aligned with high school curricula, they are not necessarily better tests.

EVALUATING THE AUTHOR'S ARGUMENTS:

In the last paragraph of the viewpoint you have just read, the author briefly mentions three arguments against standardized tests that have not been brought up previously: "susceptibility to coaching, examples of test score misuse, and the negative impact test score use has on educational equity." What is the impact of these additional arguments? Does their brevity and their placement at the end of the viewpoint make them more powerful, or less? Explain your answer.

Test Prep Courses Are a Good Investment

Scott Jaschik

"The money is worth it, especially when considering the merit scholarships that students are earning these days."

In the viewpoint that follows, education editor Scott Jaschik explores the controversy over whether coaches and tutors can help students earn higher scores on the SAT. He describes a report from the National Association for College Admission Counseling (NACAC) that acknowledges modest gains produced by test preparation companies, and he quotes representatives from those companies who claim that NACAC underestimates the value of their services. The fact that scores can be raised by expensive tutoring raises ethical problems for colleges, the viewpoint concludes, but all sides seem to agree that the services do raise scores. Jaschik is an editor and one of the founders of *Inside Higher Ed,* an online source of news about higher education.

Scott Jaschik, "Test Prep, to What End?" *Inside Higher Ed*, May 20, 2009. Reproduced by permission.

The extent to which the SAT is coachable has long been central to debates about the ethics of the test. After all, if tutoring programs that cost money help scores, there is an obvious issue of who will be able to afford such an advantage. For years, the College Board [owner of the SAT] insisted that the SAT was not coachable and, more recently, the board has said that gains from test prep services are modest.

Today [May 20, 2009], the National Association for College Admission Counseling is releasing an analysis on the impact of test preparation services that backs the claims of test prep companies that they do produce gains on the SAT. But the research described suggests that the gains are relatively small — gains that theoretically shouldn't matter much in admissions decisions. But NACAC also found evidence that at plenty of colleges, these kinds of gains could make a difference.

The NACAC report suggests several actions: Colleges are urged to avoid using the SAT and other tests in ways for which they aren't intended. And test takers are cautioned against expecting too much of an impact from test prep, and so are urged to be skeptical about gains and the value of these services.

Test prep companies, while largely concurring with the finding that gains are modest on average, maintain that the NACAC study may hide the extent to which some services result in major gains on the SAT, and thus may make the testing system even less equitable than the report suggests. . . .

Needless to say, those businesses have a keen interest in how NACAC describes their services. And test prep officials freely admit that they gain customers because of the perception that they are raising scores by far more than 30 or so points. But different kinds of services have different approaches to how they discuss score gain.

Test Prep Claims

The national chains tend not to promise specific gains or to quote average gains. Kaplan and Princeton Review, for example, have an agreement between them that they will quote figures only if they let their competitor examine the methodology and critique it—and under this agreement it has been years since either company quoted an average score gain. Both companies, however, boast on their Web sites that students will see scores go up and both offer forms of money-back guarantees for those who are not satisfied with score gains.

Seppy Basili, senior vice president at Kaplan, said NACAC is wise to encourage students not to trust promotions about score gains because the averages mean very little. A 150-point gain for someone on the low end of the SAT range is fairly easy to accomplish, Basili said, while a similar gain might be quite challenging for someone already near the top. "We're very careful not to use average score increase," he said.

SAT preparation books are big sellers, but their actual value in helping students get higher scores has been brought into question.

Basili also said that admissions counselors and the College Board have "a vested interest" in promoting the idea that test prep doesn't have a huge impact. "It's very uncomfortable for them because if test prep works, does everyone have equal access?"

The answer to that question is clear, he said. "The SAT favors anyone who can get test preparation."

Paul Kanarek, senior vice president at Princeton Review, agreed. He said that score claims are all over the place in terms of how they count "before" and "after" scores, who is in the pool, and so forth. At the same time, he suggested that the NACAC report understates the impact of coaching. "If we didn't raise scores in the eyes of the market place, we would not be one of the largest players in the market place," he said.

FAST FACT

Estimates of the annual revenues of test preparation companies in the United States range from $2 billion to $4 billion.

He said that this reputation comes largely from satisfied test takers. The only notable change in recent years, he said, is that the student describes satisfaction in different ways. "Ten years ago, it was 'I went up 300 points,' but now it's 'I broke 2000.' It's all about the final score."

Students Should Be Skeptical

While the dominant players shy away from explicit score gains, many others do not.

If you call Ivy Bound Test Prep, for example, the recording that greets you says you should choose it "if you are looking to raise your SAT scores 200 points or more." And the Web site says that "last year's students reported a 171.1 point increase (math and critical reading) over a previous SAT or PSAT."

Mark Greenstein, the president and founder, said he too agreed that students should be "skeptical and smart shoppers," but that there was nothing wrong with his company's claims. He said that his average is based on "diligent students," whom he defined as doing at least 90 percent of assignments and calling the help line at least once a week.

"If you do that, you are good for 150 points at least," he said. Greenstein said that he uses actual test scores for the "before" score. He also said that he updates the score average annually, so that it reflects the latest SAT.

Those who sign up for Ivy Bound's courses have gains about 10 points lower than the online figure of 171.1. The higher gains are for those who opt for private tutors, and Greenstein said it is clear that paying for such help pays off.

Expensive, but Worth It

Families pay by the hour and at least 25 hours of tutoring are needed to achieve the score gains (plus another 8 if students want help on the writing test of the SAT, too), he said. For less experienced tutors, families pay $60–$80 an hour, while veterans cost $210 an hour and the top of the line is $350 an hour.

The money is worth it, especially when considering the merit scholarships that students are earning these days, Greenstein said. He echoed the criticism of others in test prep in saying that admissions counselors "are dismissing the economic benefit of test prep." And while NACAC questioned the need for expensive services, Greenstein said

"MY S.A.T. SCORES WERE TOO LOW? THAT'S IT?"

that he sees a relationship between what students pay and their diligence and corresponding gains.

"There is an aspect of 'my Mom's paying $3,000 so I better do this right,'" he said.

[David] Hawkins [of NACAC] said that in fact admissions counselors and NACAC are "in the middle of competing interests." He said that he doesn't doubt that some test prep raises scores, even if the precise size of the gains isn't clear.

EVALUATING THE AUTHOR'S ARGUMENTS:

One of the experts quoted in the viewpoint you have just read, Mark Greenstein of Ivy Bound Test Prep, argues that students who pay more for test prep services will work harder and raise their scores higher than those who pay less, because they will feel more responsible to their parents. To what extent does that view of high school seniors match your observations of yourself and your peers?

Test Prep Courses Are Overrated

Derek C. Briggs

"Coaching has a positive effect on SAT performance, but the magnitude of the effect is small."

In the following viewpoint, researcher Derek C. Briggs reports on an extensive study he conducted on the value of preparation for college admissions exams, including the SAT and ACT. Although a great deal of research has been done in the past, he contends, much of it has been flawed. Recent evidence suggests, however, that tutoring or coaching for the standardized tests does improve scores, if only slightly. Briggs concludes that the test prep companies have no incentive to conduct formal studies on large samples of their clients, so students and their parents should consider promises of raised scores with skepticism. Briggs is chair of the research and evaluation methodology program at the University of Colorado–Boulder.

AS YOU READ, CONSIDER THE FOLLOWING QUESTIONS:
1. What typically happens to the test scores of students who retake a test, whether or not they have had tutoring, according to the author?
2. What does Briggs mean by the term "opportunity cost," as he uses it in the viewpoint?
3. According to the research conducted by high school juniors under the direction of Warren Buckleitner, as cited by the author, what is the relationship between the cost of an online test preparation service and its quality?

The premise of coaching programs is that engaging in such activities will have a positive effect on students' subsequent test performance. For students applying to selective postsecondary institutions that use SAT or ACT scores to make admission decisions, if coaching causes a significant increase in test performance, this might significantly increase the likelihood of admission. There are two key issues: First, to what extent does coaching have an effect on test performance? Second, if coaching has an effect, is it big enough to significantly increase a student's prospects for admission at a selective postsecondary institution? . . .

It is important to make a distinction between the *effect* of coaching and the observation (or claim) that students who prepare for a test in a particular way typically have large score gains. For example, companies and individual tutors that offer coaching for the SAT routinely promise (or imply) that their customers will increase their combined test section scores from a previous administration of the exam by anywhere from 100 points or more. Whether such promises are accurate is itself doubtful. Regardless, the question of interest would not be whether students increase their scores from one testing to the next, but whether such an increase can be validly attributed to the coaching that preceded it. In general, to make such an attribution requires the availability of a comparable group of students that take the test twice but are not coached. If the score gains of coached students are significantly larger than the score gains of uncoached students, this would constitute a positive coaching effect. Since uncoached students will on average also improve their scores just by retaking the test, an estimate of the effect of coaching will always be smaller than the observed score gains for coached students. . . .

The Effects of Admission Test Preparation

Since 1953, there have been more than 30 studies conducted to evaluate the effect of coaching on specific sections of the SAT, and two studies conducted to evaluate the effect with respect to the ACT. . . . The reviews of coaching and its effect on SAT performance have been almost as numerous as the individual studies under review. Fourteen reviews . . . have been conducted on subsets of these studies between 1978 and 2005. While one might assume from this that the empirical effectiveness of coaching on SAT performance has been well-established, this is only somewhat true. One principal reason for this is that the vast

Many people think that SAT preparatory books and computer programs are ineffective and expensive, thus putting poor and minority students at a disadvantage.

majority of coaching studies conducted over a 40 year period between 1951 and 1991 tended to involve small samples that were not necessarily representative of the national population of high school seniors taking college admission exams, and of the programs offering test coaching. In addition, a good number of these studies contained a variety of methodological flaws that compromised the validity of their conclusions.

Nonetheless, over the past 10 years evidence has emerged from three large-scale evaluations of coaching that point to a consensus position about its average effects on admission exams. This consensus is as follows:

- Coaching has a positive effect on SAT performance, but the magnitude of the effect is small.
- The effect of coaching is larger on the math section of the exam (10–20 points) than it is for the critical reading section (5–10 points).
- There is mixed evidence with respect to the effect of coaching on ACT performance. Only two studies have been conducted. The most recent evidence indicates that only private tutoring has a small effect of .4 points on the math section of the exam. . . .

The Costs of Test Preparation

Beyond that which occurs naturally during students' years of schooling, the only free test preparation is no test preparation at all. This is because all test preparation involves two costs: monetary cost and opportunity cost. The monetary cost of test preparation is relatively transparent. Practice items and tests for student-driven preparation from the SAT and ACT are available online for no cost or in books for a nominal cost (between $10 and $20). Commercial coaching is available for a considerable cost ($400 online, $1,100 for a physical class, $100–200 per hour for in-person tutoring). In contrast, opportunity cost depends upon the duration of test preparation. Any time spent preparing for an admission exam is time that could have otherwise been spent doing other sorts of activities that might either improve students' chances of college admission or better prepare them for the challenges that await once they matriculate. Hence test preparation with low opportunity cost will tend to constrain the number of hours students spend, while test preparation with high opportunity cost does not. . . .

In 2004 a group of students was asked, "To prepare for the SAT and/or ACT, did you do any of the following?: A. Take a special course at your high school; B. Take a course offered by a commercial test preparation service; C. Receive private one-to-one tutoring; D. Study from test preparation books; E. Use a test preparation computer program."

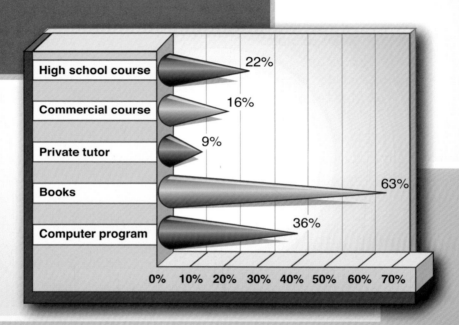

High school course	22%
Commercial course	16%
Private tutor	9%
Books	63%
Computer program	36%

0% 10% 20% 30% 40% 50% 60% 70%

Taken from: Derek C. Briggs, "Preparation for College Admissions Exams," National Association for College Admission Counseling, NACAC Discussion Paper, 2009.

The fastest growing market for commercial test preparation is in the online environment. In a study conducted for Consumer Reports WebWatch, [Warren] Buckleitner (2006) recruited 20 high school juniors to evaluate 10 online SAT test preparation services over a four week period. Students were randomly assigned to evaluate two Internet-based services each, and their progress and experiences were monitored by adult researchers. The key findings reported by Buckleitner were as follows:

- Online services come with aggressive advertising. Students may be inundated with messages from college and military recruiters or offers for financial aid.
- In six out of 10 services, errors were found in practice tests (e.g., grammatical problems, questions with no answers, missing sections of text, etc.).
- Higher price and reputation do not necessarily make for better products. The only free service that was tested (Number2.com) performed "exceptionally well" relative to more expensive competitors (The Princeton Review, Kaplan).
- Technical issues abound. Older Web browsers may not work, and some services require the use of "cookies" which can be intrusive.
- Students' privacy protection is often unclear. Some sites were very vague about what student information would be shared and with whom.

In summary, note that there is no incentive for coaching companies to formally evaluate the effectiveness of their products as part of a controlled experiment. The actual effect of coaching that would be found when the test performance of a "treatment" group of coached students is compared to that of a "control" group of uncoached students will inevitably be smaller when contrasted with the gains of a single group of students before and after they have been coached. Given that the public appears to believe that coaching will improve scores substantially rather than marginally (despite decades of empirical evidence to the contrary), coaching companies have

FAST FACT

Two-thirds of all public colleges and universities do not have minimum grade point averages or test scores for admission.

avoided taking any action that might dispel such misconceptions. Hence when it comes to commercial coaching programs, the message is "buyer beware."

The viewpoint you have just read was prepared by an expert in quantitative analysis, but it was commissioned by the National Association for College Admission Counseling (NACAC). In the previous viewpoint, representatives of test preparation companies claimed that NACAC might wish to promote evidence that test preparation services are unreliable. Here, Derek C. Briggs claims that the test prep companies might have reasons to exaggerate their own effectiveness. How should students and parents weigh these opposing viewpoints to make smart decisions about test preparation?

Facts About Standardized Testing

What Standardized Tests Reveal

According to the 2009 Nation's Report Card, a report issued by the U.S. Department of Education based on results of the National Assessment of Educational Progress (NAEP) test:

- Students numbering 161,700, from 7,030 schools across the country, took the eighth-grade mathematics test. Of these, 34 percent were rated at or above "proficient," representing "solid academic performance."
- Mathematics scores for nine- and thirteen-year-olds in 2008 were higher than in all previous years.
- Students numbering 160,900, from 7,030 schools across the country, took the eighth-grade reading test. Of these, 32 percent were rated at or above "proficient," representing "solid academic performance."
- Reading skills have improved at all ages since 2004.

Results of the 2007 NAEP Reading Test show:

- Forty percent of Asian students scored at or above "proficient" on the eighth-grade test; 38 percent of white students, 19 percent of American Indian students, 14 percent of Hispanic students, and 12 percent of African American students scored at or above proficient.

The Cost of Testing

- According to the research firm Eduventures, Inc., states were predicted to spend almost $1.1 billion on standardized tests in the 2007–2008 school year. In 2001, before the No Child Left Behind Act (NCLB) was passed, schools spent $423 million.
- In 2007 the federal government gave states $407.6 million to help pay for standardized testing required by NCLB.
- Almost 60 million standardized tests are administered each year to meet NCLB requirements.
- According to FairTest, American schools administer more than 100 million standardized tests each year, including IQ, achievement, screening, and readiness tests.

What the Public Thinks

According to a 2009 Gallup Work and Education poll:

- When asked how the No Child Left Behind Act has affected American public school education, 21 percent said it has made it better, 45 percent said it has not made much difference, and 29 percent said NCLB has made education worse.
- Among those who rated themselves as "very familiar" with NCLB, 50 percent said it has made public education worse; 30 percent of those who rated themselves "somewhat familiar" said that it has made education worse; 14 percent of those who were "not too familiar" with NCLB said that it has made education worse.

The same poll asked participants to name the "best way to improve kindergarten through 12 grade education in the U.S." Among the respondents:

- The highest percentage, 17 percent, suggested improving the quality of teachers.
- Ten percent suggested changing to a back-to-basics curriculum.
- Six percent called for smaller class sizes.
- Four percent suggested "improved standards for testing."
- Three percent mentioned "stop the government from running schools" or "get rid of No Child Left Behind."
- One percent suggested adopting year-round schooling.

According to a May 2008 survey of Canadian parents in British Columbia, conducted by the Fraser Institute:

- Seventy percent agreed with the standardized testing policies of the Ministry of Education; 19 percent disagreed; 11 percent were undecided or had no opinion.
- Seventy-seven percent stated that parents should have the right to see test results from different schools, in order to make decisions about where to send their children; 6 percent said parents should "probably" have that right; 2 percent said they should "probably not" have the right; and 12 percent said parents should not have a right to see test results. The remaining three percent were undecided or had no opinion.

What Teachers Think

According to a March 2010 survey of more than forty thousand teachers, conducted by Scholastic and the Bill and Melinda Gates Foundation:

- Ninety-two percent responded that formative, ongoing assessment during class is "absolutely essential" or "very important" in measuring student achievement. Eighty-eight percent labeled performance on class assignments as "absolutely essential" or "very important. Only 6 percent rated district-required tests so highly, and only 3 percent rated state-required standardized tests as "absolutely essential" or "very important."
- Sixteen percent of the teachers rated state-required standardized tests as "not at all important," while 11 percent rated district-required tests as "not at all important."
- Sixty percent of the teachers said that student engagement is a "very accurate" measure of a teacher's performance; 38 percent rated it "somewhat accurate"; 2 percent rated it "not at all accurate."
- Only 7 percent of the teachers said that student grades on standardized tests are a "very accurate" measure of a teacher's performance; 62 percent said that they are "somewhat accurate"; 30 percent said that they are "not at all accurate."
- When asked to name the one thing that would most improve student achievement in American schools, 39 percent of the teachers identified increased involvement and support, 27 percent identified improved teaching method and standards, 7 percent identified standardized testing, 5 percent identified more effective teachers and administrators, and 4 percent identified increased funding.

International Testing

- The Progress in International Reading Literacy Study is a fourth grade-reading test administered every five years by the International Association for the Evaluation of Educational Achievement. Fifty-five countries are scheduled to participate in 2011.
- Fifteen-year-olds in sixty-five countries take the Programme for International Student Assessment (PISA) test in reading, math, and science. In 2006 more than five thousand students in the United States took the PISA.
- Sixty-seven countries administer the Trends in International Mathematics and Science Study (TIMSS) to fourth and eighth graders. In 2007 more than seven thousand students in the United States took the TIMSS.

Facts About College Admission Tests

According to the College Board, which administers the SAT:

- High school seniors in the class of 2009 who took the SAT numbered 1,530,128. Of these, 711,368 (46 percent) were male and 818,760 (54 percent) were female.
- From this group of seniors, 294,893 students also took one or more SAT subject tests.

According to the creators of the ACT:

- High school seniors in the class of 2009 who took the ACT numbered 1,480,469. Of these, 668,165 (45 percent) were male and 808,097 (55 percent) were female; 4,207 students did not report their gender.
- In the class of 2009, 814,713 took the optional ACT writing test.

For a 2005 study conducted by the National Association for College Admission Counseling, colleges were asked to weigh the importance of different factors in deciding whom to admit. The results:

- Seventy-four percent said that a student's grades in college prep courses and the difficulty of high school courses were of "considerable importance."
- Fifty-nine percent said that admission test scores were of "considerable importance."
- Thirty-one percent said that class rank was of "considerable importance."
- Twenty-three percent said that the application essay was of "considerable importance."
- Eight percent said that extracurricular activities were of "considerable importance."

Organizations to Contact

The editors have compiled the following list of organizations concerned with the issues debated in this book. The descriptions are derived from materials provided by the organizations. All have publications or information available for interested readers. The list was compiled on the date of publication of the present volume; the information provided here may change. Be aware that many organizations take several weeks or longer to respond to queries, so allow as much time as possible.

Achieve
1775 Eye St. NW, Ste. 410
Washington, DC 20006
(202) 419-1540
fax: (202) 828-0911
Website: www.achieve.org

Created in 1996 by the nation's governors and corporate leaders, Achieve is an independent, bipartisan, nonprofit educational reform organization that helps states raise academic standards and graduation requirements, improve assessments, and strengthen accountability. In 2006 Achieve was named by *Education Week* as one of the most influential education groups in the nation. Its website describes the benchmarks Achieve has drawn up for math, English, and communication, showing what students should learn in each grade—kindergarten through high school—and includes a profile of each state's progress toward achievement goals. Achieve also publishes reports on preparing all students for college and careers, with titles including "Measures That Matter" and "Aligned Expectations? A Closer Look at College Admissions and Placement Tests," available on its website.

ACT
500 ACT Dr.

PO Box 168
Iowa City, IA 52243-0168
Website: www.act.org

ACT, the creator of the ACT, the test for high school achievement and college admission, and other standardized tests, is an independent not-for-profit organization that provides a broad array of assessment and research in the areas of education and workforce development. Its website offers information for teachers, policy makers, and students, including a student-written blog, policy reports, case studies, and issue briefs, including "Using ACT Data as Part of a State Accountability System," "Ready for College and Ready for Work: Same or Different?" and "Are High School Grades Inflated?"

Alliance for Excellent Education
1201 Connecticut Ave. NW, Ste. 901
Washington, DC 20036
(202) 828-0828
fax: (202) 828-0821
Website: www.all4ed.org

The Alliance for Excellent Education is a national policy and advocacy organization that works to improve national and federal policy so that all students can achieve at high academic levels and graduate high school ready for success in college, work, and citizenship in the twenty-first century. The alliance focuses on those secondary school students who are most likely to leave school without a diploma or to graduate unprepared for a productive future. Its website offers briefs, reports, and fact sheets intended for policy makers, education organizations, businesses, administrators, teachers, parents, and students as well as a biweekly newsletter, *Straight A's.*

American Evaluation Association (AEA)
16 Sconticut Neck Rd. #290
Fairhaven, MA 02719
(888) 232-2275
e-mail: info@eval.org
Website: www.eval.org

The AEA is an international professional association of evaluators devoted to the application and exploration of program evaluation, personnel evaluation, technology, and many other forms of evaluation. The AEA works to improve evaluation practices and methods in many areas, including prekindergarten through high school education. Publications available on its website include the 2002 "AEA Public Statement on High Stakes Testing" and the 2006 "AEA Public Statement on Educational Accountability."

College Board
45 Columbus Ave.
New York, NY 10023
(212) 713-8000
Website: www.collegeboard.com

Founded in 1900, the College Board is a not-for-profit membership association whose mission is to connect students to college success and opportunity. Among its best-known programs are the SAT, the PSAT/NMSQT, and the Advanced Placement Program. Its website provides information for students, parents, and educators, including original research reports such as "Examining the Accuracy of Self-Reported High School Grade Point Average."

Education Equality Project (EEP)
895 Broadway, 5th Fl.
New York, NY 10003
(212) 253-2021
e-mail: info@educationequalityproject.org
Website: www.edequality.org

The EEP is a civil rights organization working to eliminate the racial and ethnic achievement gap in public education by helping to create an effective school for every child. The EEP supports test-based accountability, advanced course taking, and college attendance. Its website includes information about the achievement gap in different states, as well as fact sheets, videos, blogs, and a link to the *Daily News Roundup*, a daily e-mail of education reform news.

Education Sector
1201 Connecticut Ave. NW, Ste. 850
Washington, DC 20036
(202) 552-2840
fax: (202) 775-5877
Website: www.educationsector.org

Education Sector is an independent nonprofit, nonpartisan think tank that challenges conventional thinking in education policy. Its mission is to promote changes in policy and practice that lead to improved student opportunities and outcomes, focusing on K–12 accountability, educational choice, teacher quality, and undergraduate education. Reports and articles archived on the website include *Moving Targets: What It Now Means to Make Adequate Yearly Progress Under NCLB* and "Is Data the Cure-All?"

National Board on Educational Testing and Public Policy (NBETPP)
Lynch School of Education
Boston College
Chestnut Hill, MA 02467
(617) 552-4521
fax: (617) 552-8419
e-mail: nbetpp@bc.edu
Website: www.bc.edu/research/nbetpp

The NBETPP, housed in the School of Education at Boston College, is an independent organization that monitors testing in the United States. The board provides ongoing information on the uses and outcomes of educational testing for decision-making purposes, paying special attention to groups historically underserved by the educational system. Research reports and statements available for download from its website include *Perceived Effects of State-Mandated Testing Programs on Teaching and Learning: Findings from a National Survey of Teachers* and *High Stakes Testing and High School Completion.*

National Center for Education Statistics (NCES)
1990 K St. NW
Washington, DC 20006

(202) 502-7300
Website: http://nces.ed.gov

The NCES is the primary federal entity for collecting and analyzing data related to education in the United States and other nations. The NCES is located within the U.S. Department of Education and the Institute of Education Sciences. The center collects data from many sources covering all areas of education, including elementary/secondary education, post-secondary education, and international assessments. Its website provides a massive collection of reports, fact sheets, and other publications for general readers as well as databases and other tools for use by researchers.

National Center for Fair and Open Testing (FairTest)
15 Court Sq., Ste. 820
Boston, MA 02108
(857) 350-8207
fax: (857) 350-8209
Website: www.fairtest.org

The National Center for Fair & Open Testing, otherwise known as Fair-Test, advances quality education and equal opportunity by promoting fair, open, valid, and educationally beneficial evaluations of students, teachers, and schools. FairTest also works to end the misuses and flaws of testing practices that impede those goals, placing special emphasis on eliminating the racial, class, gender, and cultural barriers to equal opportunity posed by standardized tests and preventing their damaging of the quality of education. The website archives the organization's quarterly newsletter, *Examiner*, and also includes fact sheets and organizing tools for statewide and national action campaigns.

Rand Education
The RAND Corporation
1776 Main St.
PO Box 2138
Santa Monica, CA 90407-2138
Website: www.rand.org/education

The Rand Corporation, of which Rand Education is a branch, is a global think tank originally established to conduct research for the

U.S. military. Rand Education helps policy makers assess the performance of the nation's education system by evaluating large-scale tests and exploring new approaches for measuring student achievement, establishing ways to compare the performance of students across states and internationally, and interpreting trends in student test scores. Rand posts many of its assessment reports, including *Designing Effective Pay-for-Performance in K–12 Education* and *Using Test-Score Data in the Classroom* on its website.

U.S. Department of Education

400 Maryland Ave. SW
Washington, DC 20202
(800) USA-LEARN 872-5327
Website: http://ed.gov

The U.S. Department of Education is the agency of the federal government that establishes policy for, administers, and coordinates most federal assistance to education. The department's mission is to serve America's students—to promote student achievement and preparation for global competitiveness by fostering educational excellence and ensuring equal access. The department collects data and oversees research, identifies major issues and problems in American education, and shares its findings with Congress, educators, and the general public through speeches, reports, and the annual Nation's Report Card. Its website includes research and best practices, facts and figures, press releases, transcripts of speeches, and much more.

Books

Au, Wayne. *Unequal by Design: High-Stakes Testing and the Standard-ization of Inequality.* New York: Routledge, 2009. Traces the history of high-stakes standardized testing back to the eugenics movement, showing that the testing was designed to foster inequality and continues to do so.

Baker, Joan M. *Achievement Testing in U.S. Elementary and Secondary Schools.* New York: Peter Lang, 2008. An overview of testing geared toward parents, new teachers, and policy makers.

Dolezalek, Holly, and Robyn Lea Sayre. *Standardized Testing in Schools.* Edina, MN: ABDO, 2009. An overview that presents the arguments for and against testing in K–12 education.

Farley, Todd. *Making the Grades: My Misadventures in the Standardized Testing Industry.* Sausalito, CA: PoliPoint, 2009. A veteran of scoring and developing standardized tests for K–12 education reveals how testing companies manipulate scores to achieve expected data.

Hursh, David W. *High-Stakes Testing and the Decline of Teaching and Learning: The Real Crisis in Education.* Lanham, MD: Rowman & Littlefield, 2008. Examines how educational policy in the United States and Great Britain has been altered by testing over the past twenty-five years.

Koretz, Daniel M. *Measuring Up: What Standardized Testing Really Tells Us.* Cambridge, MA: Harvard University Press, 2008. A Harvard professor explains how to interpret and use test data, using clear language intended for those with little mathematical background.

Madaus, George F., Michael K. Russell, and Jennifer Higgins. *The Paradoxes of High Stakes Testing: How They Affect Students, Their Parents, Teachers, Principals, Schools, and Society.* Cambridge, MA: Harvard University Press, 2009. Demonstrates that testing provides important information for teachers and schools but often leads to program changes that harm students.

Mathison, Sandra, and E. Wayne Ross. *The Nature and Limits of Standards-Based Reform and Assessment: Defending Public Schools.* New York: Teachers College, 2008. Thirteen essays examine the history, uses, and effectiveness of the standards-based educational reform movement.

Perlstein, Linda. *Tested: One American School Struggles to Make the Grade.* New York: Henry Holt, 2007. An in-depth look at how one Maryland school, populated mostly by low-income and minority students, worked to maintain Adequate Yearly Progress.

Phelps, Richard D. *Kill the Messenger: The War on Standardized Testing.* Piscataway, NJ: Transaction, 2008. An educational researcher argues in favor of testing and uncovers the ideological and political underpinnings of much of the criticism.

Popham, W. James. *Testing! Testing! What Every Parent Should Know About School Tests.* Needham Heights, MA: Allyn and Bacon, 2000. An accessible explanation of the different tests and what they tell— and do not tell—parents and educators.

Ravitch, Diane. *The Death and Life of the Great American School System: How Testing and Choice Are Undermining Education.* New York: Basic Books, 2009. A former U.S. assistant secretary of education rejects her own earlier faith in standardized testing and calls for neighborhood schools with a back-to-basics curriculum.

Swope, Kathy, and Barbara Miner. *Failing Our Kids: Why the Testing Craze Won't Fix Our Schools.* Milwaukee: Rethinking Schools, 2000. A collection of over fifty essays and articles on standardized testing and alternative assessments.

Tankersley, Karen. *Tests That Teach: Using Standardized Tests to Improve Education.* Alexandria, VA: Association for Supervision and Curriculum Development, 2007. Written by a teacher to provide other teachers with strategies to help students learn the useful skills that standardized tests attempt to measure.

Periodicals and Internet Sources

Baker, Keith. "Are International Tests Worth Anything?" *Phi Delta Kappan*, October 2007.

Bracey, Gerald. "Big Tests: What Ends Do They Serve?" *Educational Leadership,* November 2009.

Buddy, Juanita. "Standardized Testing Review 101," *School Library Monthly*, December 2009.

Calefati, Jessica. "Catching Students Before They Fall Behind," *U.S. News & World Report,* January 2010.

Caperton, Gaston. "Test Data Allow Better Decisions," *U.S. News & World Report,* September 2009.

Ferguson, Sue. "How Grades Fail Our Kids," *Maclean's,* January 12, 2004.

Ferreira, Jose. "A Short History of Standardized Test Preparation," *Huffington Post,* February 10, 12, and 16, 2010. www.huffington post.com.

Gasoi, Emily. "How We Define Success: Holding Values in an Era of High Stakes Accountability," *Schools: Studies in Education,* Fall 2009.

Gootman, Elissa, and Robert Gebeloff. "Gains on Tests Don't Silence School Critics," *New York Times,* August 4, 2009.

Greenblatt, Alan. "Standardizing the Standards," *Governing,* December 2009.

Hirsch, E.D., Jr. "Using Tests Productively," *Educational Horizons,* Winter 2007.

Hoover, Eric. "The Revised SAT: No Better, No Worse at Its Job," *Chronicle of Higher Education,* June 27, 2008.

Kaplan, David A. "The Standardized-Test Smackdown," *Fortune,* December 7, 2009.

Navarrette, Ruben, Jr. "Reassessing Assessment Tests: A Matter of Accountability," *Hispanic,* May 2007.

Nichols, Sharon L., and David C. Berliner. "Why Has High Stakes Testing So Easily Slipped into Contemporary American Life?" *Education Digest,* December 2008.

Padron, Eduardo J. "Reassessing Assessment Tests: What Did Johnny Really Learn Today?" *Hispanic,* May 2007.

Quellmalz, Edys S., and James W. Pellegrino. "Technology and Testing," *Science,* January 2, 2009.

Sawchuk, Stephen. "Quality of Questions on Common Tests at Issue," *Education Digest,* May 2010.

Teare, Chris. "The Russian Roulette of SAT Scores," *Chronicle of Higher Education,* May 15, 2009.

Tiefenthaler, Jill. "A Student Is More than Numbers," *U.S. News & World Report,* September 25, 2009.

Turner, Steven L. "Ethical and Appropriate High-Stakes Test Preparation in Middle School: Five Methods That Matter," *Middle School Journal,* September 2009.

Turner, Susannah. "Interpreting Test Scores: More Complicated than You Think," *Chronicle of Higher Education,* August 15, 2008.

Urbina, Ian. "States Lower Test Standards for Diploma," *New York Times,* January 12, 2010.

Vetter, Joseph K. "Quick Study: Standardized Tests," *Reader's Digest,* March 2009.

Visone, Jeremy D. "The Validity of Standardized Testing in Science," *American Secondary Education*, Fall 2009.

Wherry, John H. "Getting Parent Support for Standardized Test Success," *Principal*, November/December 2007.

Wilson, Mark. "Assessment from the Ground Up," *Phi Delta Kappan*, September 2009.

Websites

Education Commission of the States (www.ecs.org). Articles, reports, and databases about K–12 and postsecondary education in forty-nine states, three territories, and the District of Columbia.

Education Next (http://educationnext.org). Research and opinion about school reform, sponsored by the Hoover Institution at Stanford University, the Harvard Kennedy School of Government, and the Thomas B. Fordham Institute. Includes the online journal *EducationNext*, a blog, and multimedia archives.

Ericae.net Clearinghouse on Assessment and Evaluation (http://ericae .net). A virtual library of more than five hundred books and articles providing balanced information concerning educational assessment and resources to encourage responsible test use. The most complete testing website.

GreatSchools (www.greatschools.org). Offers information about the performance of individual schools so parents can make sound school-choice decisions. Also includes information and activities to help parents and educators teach and assess students.

Students Against Testing (www.nomoretests.com). Sponsored by a national network of students, the site offers discussion boards, posters, quotations, and suggestions for actions young people can take to stop high-stakes testing.

Index

Picture Credits

AP Images/Brian Chilson, 64
AP Images/Ted S. Warren, 72
David R. Frazier/Photo Researchers, Inc., 13
Melanie Stetson Freeman/The Christian Science Monitor/Getty Images, 52
Gale/Cengage Learning, 15, 19, 31, 44, 53, 66, 70, 82, 95, 104, 108, 122
Kari Goodnough/Bloomberg via Getty Images, 25
Spencer Grant/Photo Researchers, Inc., 10
Joshua Gunter/The Plain Dealer/Landov, 89
John Nordell/The Christian Science Monitor via Getty Images, 101, 109
Picture Partners/Photo Researchers, Inc., 86
Ellen B. Senisi/Photo Researchers, Inc., 38
© Ian Shaw/Alamy, 76
© Steve Skjold/Alamy, 33
Justin Sullivan/Getty Images, 114
Mario Tama/Getty Images, 120
Margaret Thomas/The Washington Post/Getty Images, 46
Kristoffer Tripplaar/UPI/Landov, 58
Jim Weber/The Commercial Appeal/Landov, 49
Roger L. Wollenberg/UPI/Landov, 97